Ministry of Agriculture

2

Ducks and Geese

Any reference to proprietary products in this book should not be construed as an official endorsement of those products, nor is any criticism implied of similar products which are not mentioned.

ISBN 0 11 240323 9

Foreword

DIVERSITY of size and colour make ducks and geese valuable as food and as ornamental birds. With greater availability brought about by better distribution and marketing they now make a significant contribution to variety in our diets. This book is mainly concerned with commercial duck and geese production but some information on ornamental varieties is included.

Mr H R Wyeld and Mrs H Wyeld are the main authors of this completely revised edition with contributions from Mr C M Groom, Mr C M Hann and for the section on maintaining health, Dr E A Gibson.

John Calvert,
Senior Poultry Husbandry Advisory Officer,
Agriculture Development and Advisory Service.

February 1979.

Ministry of Agriculture, Fisheries and Food

Acknowledgement of illustrations

THE plates in this book were reproduced from photographs kindly supplied by:
Lt-Col A A Johnson, Priory Farm, Ixworth, Suffolk.
L C Turnill, Little Gore, Gondhurst, Kent.
Messrs S B Vincent Ltd, Wramplingham Hall, Wymondham, Norfolk. (taken
by a Ministry photographer).

Contents

Present trends

Ducks and geese have a long history as established members of the farmers' livestock. Both have continued to decline in numbers in the last few decades. In the middle 1930s the June census indicated the duck population of England and Wales to be about 2·5 million whereas in the middle 1970s it stood at 1·2 million. Similarly, geese had declined from 600 000 to just over 100 000 in 1975.

The reduction in the duck population must largely be attributed to the decline in demand for duck eggs, very occasional cases of food poisoning in humans having been traced to Salmonella infection which may have originated from this source. Nevertheless there is still a market for duck eggs, and with the highly productive strains available it is possible for them to be extremely competitive with hen eggs. There should be no danger from Salmonella if they are produced in clean conditions and properly washed before sale.

The decline in the number of commercial laying ducks has been to a certain extent offset by an increase in the numbers of table ducks produced. Total production of the latter was estimated to be in the region of seven million in 1975.

The modern table duck is fast growing, achieving, under good management and housing, a liveweight of 2·9–3·2 kg at seven weeks of age with a feed conversion ratio of 3:1 or better. Figures of 2·75:1 are now being consistently achieved by progressive producers. In the last five years intensification has led to improvements in both body-weight gain and feed conversion efficiency. The body-weight of seven-week-old ducks kept intensively is comparable to the eight-week-old birds maintained under extensive conditions. This is partly due to the fact that feed conversion becomes progressively poorer with each week of age. On the conversion figures mentioned the duck cannot compete with the broiler on price; nevertheless to gourmets, ducks and indeed geese, are still attractive. In view of this, those considering large-scale production should ensure that they have a reliable market. Among helpful developments has been the increase in the number of 'steak bars' which offer duck on the menu and could stimulate demand.

Geese have an advantage over other species of poultry in that their feed costs are remarkably low if correctly managed. Goslings from the age of about four weeks thrive and fatten almost entirely on grass, making them an attractive proposition in view of the high proportion of total cost represented by feed. This characteristic can be exploited to the full if the young geese which are killed in September can be put into cold storage ready for the Christmas trade.

1

Specialisation

In terms of numbers, ducks and geese together form less than 1·5 per cent of the total national output of table poultry production, thus their economic significance has not prompted much investigational work in the fields of nutrition, genetics and embryology and for this reason knowledge is somewhat limited.

In the last five years a few large-scale operators have made some progress. Most breeding ducks are now kept intensively and increasing numbers are being fattened in controlled environment houses on litter, wire floors or slats. This results in a considerable saving of feed, not only by excluding wild birds which used to be such a problem under the open field fattening system, but by allowing the ducklings to make full use of their feed for growing and fattening instead of partially using it to maintain body temperature during cold weather. Considerable strides are now being made in egg production and hatchability with the modern *Pekin* type table duck.

Scope for further processing and luxury specialities

In the United Kingdom a pâté industry using goose livers is developing.

The special feeding techniques employed to achieve large livers for pâté production require a high standard of husbandry management and particular care must be taken to avoid unnecessary pain or distress. Producers considering such production are therefore advised to seek professional guidance (husbandry and veterinary). The production of pâté might prove to be a profitable enterprise for farmers with an aptitude for goose rearing, who can establish a market for this highly profitable product.

Anyone with the ability and resources might find it worthwhile to do some genetic research into breeding a strain of goose with an especially large liver.

At least one large-scale duck producer has developed a market for pâté made from duck livers, while others are now producing jointed birds in an effort to stimulate sales.

Ornamental water fowl

Today when economics influence the greater part of human effort, aesthetic attractions figure less in farming enterprises, so it is a pleasure to turn to one aspect of the management of ducks and geese where beauty of form is all important. In the breeding of ornamental water fowl, all effort is directed towards visual appearance and breed type. The plumage of some of these birds is magnificent and the linking of the word 'ornamental' to water fowl is amply justified.

Ducks

Table varieties

Aylesbury

WHITE ducks have been known for centuries in many countries, and as white-feathered ducks sometimes appear as sports* from darker-coloured breeds, it is thought that this may have been the origin of the *Aylesbury* (Plate III). Its present characteristics have been established by domestication and selective breeding, and it was named during the early 19th century, when large-scale duck breeding was widely carried out in the Vale of Aylesbury in Buckingham-shire. Plumage of both sexes is white, the legs and feet bright orange, the bill of the utility *Aylesbury* is often yellow and differs in shape from the exhibition bird, whose bill is pinky-white or flesh coloured. The standard weight for adult drakes is 4·5 kg and for ducks 4·0 kg.

This breed was for many years regarded as the *de luxe* table bird since it was light in the bone with a high percentage of flesh. Egg production in the *Aylesbury* was improved by selection and probably more recently by the introduction of *Pekin* blood.

Pekin

The *Pekin* (Plate II) originated in China where breeding has apparently been carried out for many centuries. In 1873 a flock of these birds was imported to Connecticut, USA, where the breed soon gained wide popularity. Since then the breed has served as a basis for table duck production in America. There is no positive evidence to show whether they came to England via America or direct from China. The *Pekin* tends to be smaller than the *Aylesbury*, it is generally a better layer and more fertile. Plumage is creamy-white, the flesh yellow, and bill and legs deep orange. It is well fleshed, matures quite quickly, and is now considered to be as good as the *Aylesbury*, with which it is sometimes crossed. Adult drakes weigh 4 kg and ducks around 3·6 kg. Eggs are white although odd birds lay pale blue or green eggs. Egg production in excess of 200 in 40 weeks has been obtained with a hatchability in excess of 80 per cent.

*A sport is defined as an individual exhibiting abnormal variation from the parent stock or type, especially in respect of form or colour.

3

Until a few years ago there were two other table breeds namely the *Pennine*, produced by the late Will Bradley in Lancashire, and the *White Table Duck* produced by S B Vincent in Norfolk, but both have become so scarce as to make them a rarity with no commercial significance. The same applies to the *Rouen* of French origin.

Muscovy

The *Muscovy*, *Brazilian* or *Barbary* duck is popular in Australia where work has been done to improve its table qualities. It is native of South America. First European reports of the *Muscovy* did not appear until the 16th century. There is still doubt as to whether it should be classed as a duck or a goose. It grazes like a goose and the males have no curled feathers in the tail, which distinguish the sex in other domesticated breeds of duck. There are no feathers on the face but the skin is bright red, whilst the drake has a knob on the head which gives the appearance of a crest. Neither sex has a voice, and their sole means of communication is by hissing. The incubation period is 34–36 days, as opposed to 28 days in other breeds. If a *Muscovy* is mated to another breed the progeny are sterile.

There are seven varieties: white-winged black—the most popular; white-winged blue; black; white; black-and-white; blue-and-white; pure white. The bill is yellow and black with some red, shading lighter towards the tip. The legs are yellow rather than orange.

The ducklings usually take not less than 16 weeks to mature; in many instances much longer. The flesh is dark and has rather a 'gamey' flavour. A feature of this breed is that the male is about twice the size of the female. Adult drakes usually weigh between 4·5 kg and 6·4 kg, and ducks between 2·2 kg and 3·1 kg. The eggs are white.

Egg-laying varieties

Although some breeds of duck, notably the *Khaki Campbell* (Plate III) and *Indian Runner*, are efficient egg producers, only a few flocks of laying ducks are kept in this country because of the modern preference for hens' eggs. This is probably due to the stronger flavour of duck eggs and the hazard from Salmonella infections associated with them. Thus ducks are kept almost entirely for meat production. Formerly the egg laying varieties consisted of the *Khaki Campbell*, *White Campbell*, *Dark Campbell*, *Indian Runner* and *Buff Orpington*, and of these breeds, only the *Khaki Campbell* has survived in appreciable numbers as an economic egg producer while others may appear as exhibition varieties.

The Campbell

The *Campbell* was evolved by Mrs A Campbell and introduced in 1901 as the result of crossing strains of *Fawn* and *White* runner, *Mallard* and *Rouen*. It was intended solely as a high egg producing breed. The plumage of the original duck was the colour of withered grass while the drake followed the colouring of the *Mallard* male but was rather lighter and had no white collar.

From the *Campbell*, the *Khaki Campbell* was evolved. It is a variety of the *Campbell* resulting directly from colour selection of the original *Campbell*. The female is a warm khaki throughout with head, neck and wings a slightly darker shade of khaki. The rest of the body has each feather narrowly laced with a slightly lighter shade of khaki which, on close examination, is seen to form a pattern. The drake's head, neck, stern and wing-bar plumage is a lustrous green-bronze, the remainder an even shade of warm khaki. The legs and feet of the original duck were an orange-brown, but today the *Khaki's* legs and feet should be as near to body-colour as possible. The legs and feet of the drake are orange.

The *Khaki Campbell* (Plate III) became increasingly popular during the first half of this century, particularly during the 1920s and 1930s, as successful breeders raised potential egg production considerably. Indeed, very high performances have been achieved. Individual production records of almost an egg a day for well over 12 months have not been uncommon and flocks have averaged in excess of 300 eggs per annum. Standard weights for this breed are: drakes 2·2–2·4 kg, ducks (when in lay) 2·0–2·2 kg.

Techniques associated with breeding

Artificial light

Day-length has a considerable influence on the reproductive behaviour of both ducks and geese. In general these effects appear to resemble those for the domestic fowl for which light requirements have been much more fully investigated.

As with the fowl, it is the change in day-length rather than the actual numbers of hours of light per day that has the main influence on egg production. In extreme circumstances, extended lighting may result in birds becoming unresponsive to changes in lighting pattern.

Such experiments as have been carried out suggest that 14–16 hours of light per day is adequate for maximum response. With such day-lengths satisfactory egg production can be obtained.

Breeders have shown that fertility is much improved during the winter months if the males are subjected to 17 hours light per day for two weeks before the females are brought into lay.

Restricted lighting has been tried on a commercial scale and it would seem practicable to subject the growing female to a six to eight hour day-length, followed by a jump to 11–12 hours and from then on a gradual increase to 16–17 hours. This entails costly housing but may well be worth the breeder's consideration. However if the growing stock are to be range-reared this system is not possible and the answer then lies in hatching future breeders so that the growing period coincides with a naturally shortening day-length. They can then be brought into lay as required by housing them and subjecting them to a minimum day-length of 14 hours, increasing to 17.

Artificial insemination

With a natural mating ratio of one male to no more than eight ducks, a reduction in the number of males needed might be achieved with the aid of artificial insemination. Unfortunately, despite experimental evidence indicating that neither semen collection from drakes nor the insemination of ducks is difficult, the commercial advantages of artificial insemination are dubious. The main difficulty is the need to inseminate every three days or so to maintain high fertility. Not only is the labour cost higher than with turkeys where in many cases AI is commercially advantageous, but the value of the product, the fertile egg, is considerably less. A further factor is the limited saving in the number of males needed because of the higher insemination frequency (twice to four times that required for the turkey).

If practised, artificial insemination should be carried out only by competent, trained personnel maintaining a high standard of hygiene and taking care to avoid unnecessary disturbance or injuring the ducks.

Sexing

Apart from the colour differences of the sexes that exist in some breeds and crosses, there are three methods of distinguishing between males and females:

Vent examination
At day old as soon as the ducklings are dry, the sex can be determined by examination of the vent. They should be held in the left hand with the head hanging down between the figures and the vent opened by pressing with the thumb and first finger of the right hand. The male organ can be easily seen appearing as a small projection. It is a much simpler job than with chickens and a reasonable degree of accuracy can be achieved after a little experience.

Voice
There is a considerable difference between the voices of the duck and the drake even as early as six to eight weeks. The duck has a definite 'quack' while the voice of the drake is lower pitched and slightly rougher.

Form of plumage
When the drakes have grown their adult plumage, some of the tail feathers curl while those of the female show no such tendency. This does not apply to the *Muscovy* but in this case the larger size of the drake aids sex determination.

Marking

To trace the origin of ducklings, two methods of marking can be used (Fig. 1). The first is by punching or cutting the web of the foot or feet. Each foot has two webs and there are also smaller flaps of skin along the sides. Holes can be made with a toe punch or the web can be slit by using a sharp knife, scissors or a razor blade. All incisions must be clearcut otherwise the two sides may grow together again. Although there are many combinations of markings that can be used, it is better to keep to five or six easily recognised ones as, above this number the task of sorting into different groups becomes time consuming.

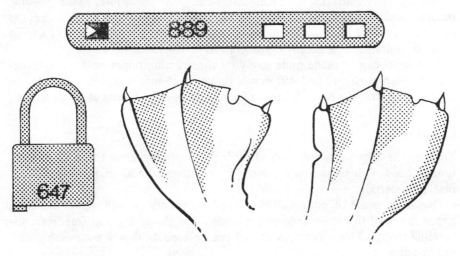

Fig. 1 Marking methods
Top: Leg band. *Lower left:* Wing tab
Lower centre and right: Web punching

If pedigree recording is involved, numbered wing bands or wing tabs are the only really effective method of identification. They are attached to the flap of skin that stretches across the inner part of the wing. This is most easily carried out as the ducklings are removed from the pedigree hatching cages. Because there is little space on the wing to insert the bands, and a number subsequently becomes detached, it is wise to place bands on both wings. In any case, wing bands should be examined when the ducklings are two weeks old as occasionally the tip of the wing gets caught up in the band, and as a result becomes damaged.

Mating systems

Breeding stock should be mated at least one month before eggs are required for hatching. The usual mating ratio for single male pens is not more than eight females to one male (egg laying strains) or four or five females and one male (table strains). Similar ratios are employed in flock matings, even though, very early in the year, males may not be quite as active as they are later on. If, as the season advances, it appears that a proportion of the ducks is getting too much attention, it is wise to remove one or more males from a breeding flock. Such action helps to reduce over-mating and saves feed costs.

Rotational mating systems may save on the numbers of drakes needed. For example, when a drake is moved systematically from one separately penned duck to another each day he can be expected to produce good results with as many as ten ducks.

Trap nesting

The traditional trap nest as used for the fowl is not very satisfactory and it is usual practice to place each duck in an individual wire cage each evening from which she is released the following morning. This procedure, made possible because ducks lay early in the morning and tend to be extremely regular, results in higher levels of accuracy than can be achieved by other methods. On a large scale, trap nesting is generally considered to be impracticable.

Trap nests can be made quite easily by constructing boxes or cages approximately 300 mm square and 450 mm high, using 25 mm wire netting stapled to light wooden frames. A single hinged lid may be used for blocks of six such nests.

Clean nests

To keep the eggs from becoming dirty it is essential to have the sides of duck houses lined with nests which should have adequate and frequently changed nesting material.

One main cause of poor hatching results is mould growth within the eggs, hence the need to ensure that nest materials are clean, dry and free from discernible mould. Floor-laid eggs should not be used as they are inevitably contaminated by dirt.

Egg collection, washing and culling

Eggs should be collected as soon as possible after they are laid to minimise moisture loss by evaporation. Not only does excessive evaporation affect hatchability because the embryo requires the correct amount of moisture, but as the contents of the egg contract, disease organisms may be drawn through the pores of the shell.

Despite endeavours to keep laying houses clean, duck eggs are frequently heavily soiled on collection, in which case their potential hatchability is usually improved by washing—infinitely preferable to leaving the soiling on the eggs with the risk of faecal and soil-borne bacteria being drawn in as they cool. Eggs should be washed or dipped in water at a higher temperature than that of the egg. Temperatures in the range 38°–60°C are normally recommended. The time of immersion should not exceed one minute if the higher temperature is used.

A number of detergent-sanitisers and disinfecting agents are available. Alternatively dairy hypochlorite may be used at a four per cent solution. In all cases it is essential to follow the manufacturer's recommendations for length of dipping time, temperature and concentration of the dip. With duck eggs the dip may rapidly become dirty. It is therefore desirable that it should be changed more frequently even than the recommendation, rather than that it should continue to be used after it has lost its disinfecting properties. Where possible a system of warm air drying helps to prevent residual contamination but hatching eggs should not be exposed to draughts.

The practice of dry cleaning duck eggs has virtually ceased as the results obtained are generally not as satisfactory as when thorough washing is carried out.

Eggs may be fumigated after they have been washed or dipped but if collected and washed efficiently there appears to be no benefit from this practice especially if they are fumigated on initial setting in the incubator.

Incubation

(For conversion of Centigrade to Fahrenheit see Appendix 2)
Satisfactory levels of hatchability can be attained from duck eggs whether they are incubated naturally (under broodies) or artificially (in incubators). Although laying may start at between five and six months of age, depending on the type of duck, the time of year at which hatching took place and possibly on the pattern of light used for rearing (although no experimental evidence is yet available), it is wise not to set eggs from stock less than 26 weeks old. This applies to both elite selected breeding flocks and those for commercial multiplication. Correct breeding procedures and good management are important. From the time eggs are laid considerable care in collection, cleaning, storage and finally incubation is essential if maximum numbers of ducklings are to hatch.

Storage and fumigation

Eggs for hatching should be stored at a temperature of between 13°–16°C with a relative humidity of 75 per cent. Under even these storage conditions there is a decline in hatchability after seven days. Eggs kept longer than seven days suffer a decline in embryonic viability and it is advisable for them to be stored in such a way that they can be turned through about 90 degrees each day. This is most easily done by using 30 dozen size egg boxes and raising alternate ends 300–375 mm. Hatching egg storage in the past has not always received the attention deserved. It is now considered that a properly designed and insulated egg storage room with facilities for keeping the temperature and humidity at precisely accurate levels, is an essential requirement in the large scale handling of duck hatching eggs. (Plate V.)

When the eggs have been trayed-up and loaded into the setter, fumigation is carried out by liberating formaldehyde vapour. This may be produced by adding 45 g ($4\frac{1}{2}$ fl oz) of formalin to 30 g (3 oz) of potassium permanganate for each 3 m³ (100 cu ft) of incubator space. The appropriate amount of permanganate should be weighed out and placed in a container* in the incubator before the formalin is added. Formalin and potassium permanganate react with violence and care must be taken when the chemicals are mixed. In particular the following precautions should be observed:

● The permanganate container should be of metal; have steep sides to prevent the reactants boiling over; and be capable of holding at least three times the amount of formalin that is to be added.
● *The formalin should always be added to the permanganate.*
● Inhalation of formaldehyde vapour should be avoided.
Fumigation should only be carried out during the first 24 hours of incubation.

*Where incubator space exceeds 200 m³ (700 cu ft), more than one container should be used and the permanganate divided equally between them.

9

Testing for defects

Before placing eggs in incubators it is usually worth candling them so that those with previously undetected hair cracks or with internal faults may be removed. Individual eggs, or those arranged on wire incubator setting trays, are passed over a strong light in a darkened room to enable defects to be seen. The most important faults are:

● Stale eggs. A larger air space than usual, the yolk being more dense with a uniform outline.
● Meat or blood spots. Red spots appear to float on the side of the yolk.
● Blood eggs. These show a greater mass of a reddish tint.
● Floating air space. Not always easy to see when candling. The white appears to have one or more bubbles floating in it which change position as the egg is moved. These bubbles are thought to result from storage at too high a temperature but some birds seem to produce sequences of eggs with floating air space.
● Double yolks. These are often produced when birds start laying. The two or more yolks are easily seen and such eggs are best discarded as they seldom hatch.

The incubator house

Points to be borne in mind are: air flow, temperature, humidity and hygiene, since all of these directly affect conditions in the incubator. Before designing the incubator house, the type of incubator should be taken into consideration and advice obtained from the manufacturer.

If an existing building is to be used, ventilators and baffled inlets may need to be installed to ensure a sufficient flow of air. The actual requirement depends on many factors including the number and size of incubators in use and whether they are running full or only partly full.

Unless ventilation is automatic, provision should be made for its manual control by the use of adjustable shutters. Care is necessary in the siting of both air inlets and doors so as to avoid the possibility of draughts around the machines.

The incubator room should be kept at a fairly even temperature between 17°–21°C. To assist in this the roof and walls should be well insulated.

Incubators vary considerably and it is advisable to follow the maker's instructions for incubating duck as opposed to hen eggs. A description is given below of the most successful method of hatching duck eggs in small 150 hen egg hot-air machines. The general principles of management apply to all duck egg hatching; correct temperature, humidity at various stages and air flow being the most important factors in the running of any make of machine.

Incubator routine

The small hot air type incubator
When using small machines, eggs of approximately the same size should be selected for each tray. Because heat comes from above in most incubators other

than force-draught cabinets, the temperature of larger eggs will always be slightly higher than that of smaller eggs on the same tray.

The following routine is generally applicable, although relating particularly to the 150 eggs size hot-air type incubator using three felts:

With the thermometer positioned so that the bottom of the bulb is just at the height of the average sized egg, the incubator should run empty at the correct running temperature as given by the makers (usually 39°C) for at least 24 hours before the eggs are placed in the machine.

The moisture pans should be filled just prior to setting, or as the eggs are set.

1st day. Eggs should be set in the morning so that the temperature can be correctly adjusted before the machine is left for the night. To avoid rapid increases in temperature, the doors of small machines should be left open for about an hour after setting.

2nd day. After setting warm water should be lightly sprinkled over the eggs once daily. From the 15th up to the end of the 23rd day, water should be sprinkled three times daily, the quantity becoming increasingly liberal.

Turning should take place twice each day, eg, at 8 am and 8 pm up to the end of the 23rd day of incubation. It is an advantage to mark the eggs with + on one side and O on the other so that it is easy to tell when the eggs have been turned through 180°.

7th and 14th days. Eggs may be candled for removal of infertile eggs and early dead embryos.

20th day. Remove one felt.

24th day. Remove second felt. Dead germs may also be removed. When pedigree breeding, the eggs should be placed in bags or cages on the 24th day.

26th day. Remove third felt or cover it with hessian.

28th day. Hatching should be completed by the end of the 28th day, although eggs that have been stored for more than five or six days may take longer.

Small incubators may be heated by paraffin lamps or electricity.

Cabinet incubators

Several manufacturers offer models specifically for hatching duck eggs though these differ little in design from those used for chicken eggs. Although some commercial operators consider that better results are achieved by setting duck eggs horizontally, others obtain good results by setting them upright in the setting trays. Both methods seem to be satisfactory. After candling and transfer on the 24th day it is normal practice to put the eggs on their sides in the hatching trays.

Air velocity, rate of air exchange between the inside and outside of an incubator, temperature and the pattern of air distribution within the machine all affect the level of humidity. It should also be remembered that different models and sometimes individual machines differ and makers' instructions must be the first guide.

There is evidence to indicate that during the period of incubation the loss of water by evaporation occurs at a considerably lower rate in duck eggs than in turkey or chicken eggs. Because of the variability in incubator design, only experience will show the best settings for the controls of a particular machine.

If the product used to wash the eggs removes the albumen deposit with which duck eggs are naturally coated a different humidity setting may be necessary, as the eggs will then suffer a greater loss of moisture by evaporation.

The following incubator temperature and wet bulb readings are suggested:

Eggs with albumen not removed

| Temperature | Wet bulb |
| 37·5°C | 31·5°C |

For eggs with the albumen removed

| Temperature | Wet bulb |
| 37·5°C | 30·6°C |

But as always the makers' instructions should be followed.

From the 24th day—on transfer to the hatcher suitable operating temperatures suggested are:

Temperature 37°C
Wet bulb 33°C

Twelve hours before taking off, the humidity should be reduced to allow the ducklings to dry off.

Candling—Testing for dead germs and infertile eggs

Duck eggs are quite easy to test by holding a strong light under a tray of eggs and looking down 'through' the eggs at the light. Eggs may be tested as early as the third or fourth day of incubation provided chilling of the eggs is avoided, however it is better to wait until the seventh day when the developing embryos can more easily be seen.

If at any time a black or blue patch shows through the shell above the air space, mould growth should be suspected. It is advisable to remove any such eggs from the incubator or store room and to verify the growth of mould by opening the shell above the air space. Eggs thus affected should be discarded immediately in such a way that the spores of the mould are not allowed to escape into the air. Other eggs should not be handled until the operator's hands have been washed. Thorough cleaning and disinfection of the incubator should be carried out after the hatch and if possible the trouble traced to its source. Mouldy floor or nest litter are frequently to blame.

Fungal spores are difficult to kill, the most effective disinfectants being the ampholytes, the quaternary ammonium compounds (non-ionic mixtures) and organic mercury compounds for persistent cases.

Some causes and results of poor hatches are given in Table 1.

Hatchery records
To run a hatchery efficiently it is essential to maintain a record of the results obtained. Such information may be conveniently entered on the chart shown opposite.

Table 1 Causes of poor hatchability

Cause	Result
Temperature too high at commencement of hatch	'Smudgy'—burst yolks; excessive number of almost clear eggs.
Temperature too high towards the end of hatch	Ducklings fully formed but fail to hatch. Embryos become very active at pipping time so temperature increases quickly. Adjustments of dampers (where these are in use) have to be made to keep the temperature down to normal. (Failure to hatch can be inherited).
Humidity too low at hatching time.	Ducklings start to pip but die; the bill of a dead duckling protrudes through a single hole; ducklings that do hatch have pieces of shell sticking to them and the ducklings tend to hatch late.
Humidity too high at hatching time.	Ducklings fully formed but die before pipping; these appear slimy as do those that actually hatch, and the ducklings tend to hatch early.
Temperature too low throughout hatch.	The hatch extended beyond the normal 28 days.
Temperature a little too high throughout hatch.	Ducklings hatch early.

Date Set..

Pen No.	Number set	Infertile	Dead germs	Removed at 2nd test	Dead in shell	Duckling hatched	Per cent hatch of all eggs set

In the case of pedigree breeding programmes the information should also be related to the parents producing the eggs, and a record must be maintained of the wing or leg band numbers allocated to the ducklings which hatch.

Nutrition

Breeding stock

A diet for breeding stock must be adequate to ensure both the health of the parent birds and high production of settable eggs. It is important that these eggs are highly fertile and hatchable to produce ducklings that grow well to fulfil their genetic potential.

Little research has been done in the United Kingdom on the nutrition of the breeding duck, and feeding is based mainly on experience with certain rations and a knowledge gained from other species of poultry.

Ducks should be fed the breeding diet at least four weeks before hatching eggs are required. While grain balancer rations may sometimes have their place, they are not generally recommended, and a balanced pelleted breeder ration is the best feeding method to adopt. Feed intake varies according to breed, body-weight, egg production and availability of grass, but will usually range from 170–230 g per day.

It is necessary to restrict feed availability so that if the ducks are let out on grass runs during the day they should have no feed provided outside but if kept entirely inside, feed hoppers should be closed for at least 12 hours a day—otherwise they may become over fat particularly the heavier table type of breeder.

A suitable ration for breeding ducks is given in Table 2. It is calculated to contain 17·0 per cent crude protein, 3·1 per cent calcium with a metabolisable energy (ME) content of 2694 k cals/kg.

Holding ration

Holding rations may be required for (a) stock breeding ducks between 8 and 20 weeks of age and (b) breeding ducks being moulted between lays. These rations should vary slightly in formulation, the young stock requiring rather more protein and calcium and where good grass is available the adults needing little more than a cereal-based feed with vitamins and trace minerals added. Where little or no grass is available a somewhat more balanced ration will be required so that stock of both kinds may build up reserves for future laying requirements. A holding ration subject to the above adjustments can be seen in Table 2.

Growing stock

The growth potential of the modern table duckling requires good feeding so that it may be fully exploited, and pelleting of the feed is essential. The starter feed should be in pellet size of 3 mm while from two weeks, 5 mm pellets would be suitable. Rapid gains require high intake, and feed must be made available in troughs so designed that the duck can easily 'shovel it in'. Plenty of clean drinking water is essential.

Vitamin and trace nutrient supplements for duck rations should contain A D_3, B_2, B_{12} and Niacin. In general, where simple formulations are involved a more complete vitamin pre-mix is usually desirable. This would contain, in

Table 2 Duck diets (kg/t mix)

	Starter	Grower	Finisher	Breeder	Holding ration
Wheat meal (coarse)	500	423	600	433	800
Maize meal (fresh)	267	329	300	300	—
Barley meal (fine)	—	100	—	—	165
Fish meal	113	50	31	67	—
Soya bean meal	100	54	—	67	—
Meat-and-bone meal	8	25	50	33	22
Grass meal	—	—	—	33	—
Limestone (flour or granules)	10	10	10	60	—
Dicalcium phosphate	—	7	—	—	—
Fat	—	—	6	—	—
Supplement (Vit/Min)	13	13	13	13	13
Calculated Analysis					
Crude Protein %	20·2	15·5	13·3	17·0	11·3
M E kilocal/kg	2885	2877	2965	2694	2825
Ca %	1·24	1·12	0·99	3·1	0·21

addition to the vitamins listed above, Pantothenic Acid, Folic Acid, Vitamin E, Vitamin K biotin, and perhaps Choline. The mineral supplement should supply the needs for calcium, phosphorus and iodised common salt and also contain manganese and zinc. The more sophisticated pre-mixes will include copper. In the case of breeder diets and duck starter feeds, complete vitamin and trace element pre-mixes are essential.

Energy

A considerable range of energy levels has been shown to give satisfactory results for table duckling but it is advisable to keep the breeders ration below about 2700 k cal/kg. A finisher ration should not be far below 3000 k cal/kg and starter and grower rations between the two. If fed too high an energy ration with a protein content higher than those shown in Table 2 above there is a danger of getting an excessively fat carcase.

Protein and energy should be balanced and ratios of k cal/kg of metabolisable energy to per cent crude protein should be approximately:

140–150 for duck starter.
180–190 for duck grower.
220–225 for duck finisher.
150–160 for duck breeder.

With these ratios it is obvious that duck finisher should only be used as the name implies and for about 10–14 days. The starter is used for the first fortnight with the growers ration for the 3–3½ weeks between them.

Niacin

The vitamin niacin is important in duck feeds particularly for the prevention of leg weakness. It is naturally occurring in whole cereals although there is evidence

15

that in some cereal by-products the vitamin may not be available to the duckling and the chicken. Awareness of this fact is important and as a safety measure about five to seven per cent of brewers' yeast could be included in breeder and starter rations to improve growth and to prevent bowed legs and other leg weakness.

Iodinated casein

It has been shown that 100–150 g of iodinated casein per t of feed can give improved growth and lower fat content.

Laying duck feeding

Light breed layer ducks may be fed a diet similar to that for hybrid laying fowls, although there is no scientific basis for assuming that this would be optimum. Laying ducks giving a conversion ratio of over 2·5 kg feed per kg eggs could be fed a diet suitable for brown egg laying fowls, and those showing a feed conversion ratio of under 2·5:1 might be given one more suited to white egg layers.

Management and housing

Brooding

Ducklings intended for table or egg production are, in general, treated similarly during brooding. This period extends from day-old until the duckling requires no further heat—usually at about three weeks according to the time of year. Brooding may be either natural or artificial, but whatever system is used it should be remembered that all young stock need much attention and frequent visits are advisable. It is particularly important to check that all is well at the last visit each night.

Natural brooding
If only a few ducklings are needed they can be brooded under hens which can either hatch them from fertile eggs or be given them at day-old. The most suitable type is either a heavy breed or a heavy breed cross, as these are better sitters, better mothers and will cover more ducklings. Broody hens should be deloused with a good dusting powder. The usual wooden or metal coop only serves for a few days, as the ducklings grow rapidly and soon find difficulty in getting through the slatted front. A small house is preferable, say 1·8 × 1·2 m, which can still be used after the hen is taken away.

A large broody hen covers about eleven eggs or takes 10–15 ducklings. This may seem rather a large number but after a few days the ducklings need only a little heat, and may not even sit under her very much. The floor may be covered with sawdust, peat-moss, chaff or short cut straw and renewed daily. Feed and water should be placed in the house for the first few days and then taken outside.

To prevent them from wandering, a surround of some kind, such as wire netting, should be used. After two to three weeks they need no further mothering and the hen can be put back with the rest of the laying flock.

When large numbers are required artificial brooding is the only practical and economic method to adopt.

Artificial brooding

The ducklings should be taken from the incubator as soon as they are dry and kept at a temperature of 29°–32°C for the first few days. The temperature is then reduced by about 3°C every two to three days according to the weather. During the summer it can be cut off altogether at eight to ten days old, but in cold weather it may have to be continued for longer. Artificial brooding is normally based on hot water, gas or electricity in conjunction with canopies or with single or multi-tiered cages.

With floor systems it is important to prevent baby ducklings from wandering too far from the source of heat (Plate VI). To prevent this and to minimise floor draughts a surround of some kind should be used. Materials such as oil tempered hardboard or flat galvanised sheeting are suitable as they can be thoroughly cleaned and disinfected between each batch. Alternatively corrugated cardboard may be used. A dim light also helps to curb wandering as well as reducing the tendency for the ducklings to crowd.

Infra-red

The advantages of this system are that it is cheap to install and easy to run. The tendency to overcrowd is not nearly so great. There are several types available: the bright and dull electric emitters and those heated by gas. The choice is to some extent a matter of personal preference, although it is thought that the output of bright emitters destroys certain vitamins in the feed. As a precaution hoppers should be placed away from direct rays. The dull emitters are fitted with a pilot light to show when the heat is on. It is customary to allow 30–40 ducklings to each 250 watt bulb.

Ducklings are weaned from heat by gradually raising the lamp a few centimetres at a time. Frequency and amount depends on the weather and the time of year, but before being cut off altogether it should first be switched off during the day and continued at night.

Infra-red heating is only satisfactory in houses that are well constructed and insulated as the system affords no protection of any kind against draughts. Unless this is realised high losses can occur.

Canopies

The old method of brooding with hovers and using paraffin as a source of heat is now seldom used. A modern version of this equipment known as a canopy (and heated by gas or electricity) has replaced it. The canopy is normally suspended, as opposed to being free-standing, and is generally larger, usually accommodating not less than 500 ducklings. This method has become very popular with many of the large scale rearers.

Raised wire floor brooding

This is quite a popular method of brooding. It involves the use of 12 mm sq welded-mesh wire mounted on brick or concrete block walls with a gas canopy suspended overhead (Plate VII). There is frequently an outside run which can be used for hardening the ducklings off before they are removed to the fattening quarters.

The brooder house

The house can be of concrete blocks, brick or timber. If large-scale production is envisaged it is recommended that the house be windowless, fully insulated and fitted with heating and fan assisted ventilation capable of giving a controlled environment (see your ADAS adviser for further information). The floor may be covered with wood shavings or other suitable material (Plate VI).

Where the failure of any mechanical or electrical automated equipment could cause distress to the birds, an automatic alarm system is essential to warn of breakdown. It is advisable to have an emergency method of ventilation for use in the event of failure of the mechanical or electrical systems. Consideration should be given to the installation of an automatic fail-safe system to give alternative ventilation. A stocking density for duckling of $14/m^2$ to three weeks of age is recommended. Alternatively the whole floor area can be of a 12 mm, eight gauge, welded-mesh wire raised floor, above a concrete floor sloping towards a central gulley, so that cleaning down can be carried out with a pressure washer and without the necessity for removing the wire sections (Plate VII). In this case 25 ducklings/m^2 to three weeks of age may be allowed. In either case careful thought must be given to the disposal of the wash-down effluent.

Whether large or small numbers are kept, wire floor rearing and fattening has much to commend it. Prejudice against this method has largely disappeared and it is extremely successful for brooding to three weeks. In fact many operators, by careful attention to detail, are making a success of continuing it right through to killing at seven to eight weeks of age. Obvious advantages are a saving of labour, litter and land and an improvement in feed conversion efficiency. Furthermore there is no loss of feed to wild birds and other vermin. Such a unit can be operated in one of two ways—in the first method one could allow 18 ducklings/m^2 for brooding to three weeks of age and then remove the ducklings either to grass runs or, more commonly to a fattening house. Alternatively, allowing six ducklings/m^2 it can be used as a brooding and fattening unit taking the ducks through to seven or eight weeks of age when they are killed.

As ducks drink much water their droppings are very wet. They also spill a considerable amount and the provision of a wire or slatted drinking platform with a drainage channel is advisable when a solid floor system is used.

If continuous production is envisaged it may be convenient to build a brooder house on the end of each fattening house. In a seven-week production cycle the brooder house would be empty for one week thus allowing time for cleaning and disinfecting.

In all cases it is important to allow ample trough and drinker space. Recommended allowances are:

	Per 100 ducks	
	Feeding space	Drinking space
Day old to 8 weeks	0·5 m	0·5 m
8 weeks and over	0·6 m	0·6 m

If only small numbers of ducklings are being produced natural ventilation from windows and ridge outlets is satisfactory.

The value of controlled lighting for ducks has still to be proven but it is usual to allow dim light during the hours of darkness for all housed ducks.

The siting of the brooder house is most important in view of the disease problems that duck fatteners have faced in recent years. It should be placed reasonably near to the service buildings, near to a hard road, but as far away as possible from other ducks. With such arrangement there is evidence that losses have not been as heavy as on less well-planned units. The importance of separating ducks of different ages cannot be too strongly emphasised.

Whether wire or solid floors are used it is better to keep the whole floor area clean using only temporary partitions. In this way cleaning is facilitated. Partitions need only be 450–600 mm high.

Litter materials
Wood shavings make a suitable litter material and coarse peat moss and sand are sometimes used. Pulverised pine bark, where available, has been found to make a satisfactory alternative litter. However, such litter materials are costly and both littering and litter removal very expensive. With rising labour costs there has been an appreciable swing to welded-mesh or expanded metal floors. Nevertheless, if litter is used it should be replenished in small amounts daily rather than in larger quantities at greater intervals.

Frequent checks should be made on the state of the litter. It should be prevented from becoming excessively wet or dry, or infested with parasites and harmful organisms.

Rearing/fattening (3–4 weeks onwards)

Because the objectives are different, the treatment of table ducklings differs appreciably from that of potential commercial egg producers. In the case of table duck type breeding stock, it is likely that a proportion may well be reared in the same way as fattening ducks, so that growth characteristics can be properly assessed. After eight weeks the treatment of breeding and ordinary laying stock may be quite similar.

The large scale systems used for table ducklings during the growing and finishing stages are designed to economise in labour and capital equipment. Inevitably the risks of loss due to environmental factors, especially competition and disease, tend to be greater than with the smaller scale systems usually associated with ducks for egg production. In the latter case, because of the higher unit value of the birds, it is economic to provide specialised housing.

Both for table ducks and egg production stock, the age at which the ducklings are moved outside varies with the system, but generally it is at three to four weeks. By this stage the ducklings should be sufficiently hardy, even during the winter months.

Any upset during the fattening stage has a retarding effect. If the ducklings are frightened, handled or herded together too frequently, they may become lame and have difficulty in moving. This appears to be due to a nervous condition which may or may not disappear with time.

Various kinds of vermin attack small ducklings and they are particularly vulnerable to rats and foxes. Stoats and weasels are also dangerous. Crows and certain gulls readily kill young ducklings by decapitating them. They swoop into the pen and kill quickly leaving survivors excited and frightened.

Large flock rearing

It is common practice to run not more than 400–500 ducklings per pen. Where ample light sandy land is available, ducklings undoubtedly do well in large flocks even though they may be more difficult to handle. Wire netting fences no more than 600 mm high are adequate for control. Shelter, made from corrugated iron or asbestos sheets placed over straw bales, should be provided in each pen. Such shelters from sun and storm may only be used during the first few days after which the ducklings tend to sleep in the open.

As many as 2500 ducklings per ha can be kept without detriment if the runs are changed regularly for grass recovery with reseeding when needed (Plate VI). In the past, this system has kept some of the lighter soils of East Anglia fertile but economic pressure now dictates more economic intensive systems. From a health and disease control aspect the system has something to commend it but the labour involved in moving fencing, carting equipment and thawing drinking water in winter is high. Furthermore because feed is expensive the large amounts frequently eaten by wild birds add considerably to costs.

Small flock rearing

Small numbers of ducklings can be reared successfully in grass pens and a pen of 20 m² is adequate for 90–100 ducklings up to killing. Although not essential, a house measuring 3·6 × 3 m (about 11 m²) would be suitable for this number. In fine weather the ducks often ignore accommodation provided and sleep in the open but it may provide valuable protection in bad weather. The house may be quite a low structure and completely open at the front.

With permanent housing it is advisable to have alternate runs. It is not easy to keep these in good condition as ducks like to burrow with their bills for worms, which makes the ground surface uneven. The grass should be kept short to minimise parasites. As soon as the surface looks worn, the run should be rested and the alternate run used.

Ducks can remain in the same house for fattening but it is preferable to confine them to straw yards adjoining the house. These should have a similar area to that provided in the house, in this case about 11 m². The straw should be replenished daily to keep the ducks clean and healthy.

General management—young stock

Whatever system is adopted the rearing of ducklings is not difficult provided that intelligent management is applied. The main points to remember are: adequate heat (during the brooding stage), suitable housing, a balanced diet and sufficient feed and trough space.

Table varieties

Norfolk was for many years the leading table duck producing area, but more recently the industry has undergone considerable change and expansion both in Norfolk and elsewhere.

The objective is to maximise growth to killing age while minimising feed requirement. The factors involved include killing age itself, feed composition (see Nutrition section page 14), feed wastage and the strain of duck. In addition there are seasonal effects due to the greater feed requirement to maintain the birds in winter when environmental temperatures are low, and the lesser requirement for maintenance in summer. It is these two factors and the ravages of wild birds and vermin that have helped to bring in the use of intensive housing.

Table 3 emphasises the desirability of marketing table ducks by eight weeks of age. These figures from the USA show the falling off in conversion ratios even at eight weeks. It is now common practice in the UK to kill at 46–49 days. With the current strains of improved meat type duck it is possible to obtain a liveweight of 3·2 kg at 49 days with a conversion ratio of well under 3:1.

Under winter conditions large flocks outside give much less favourable feed conversion ratios.

Apart from efficient feed conversion, other objectives to be considered are uniform growth and the attainment of low mortality. Clearly many factors are

Table 3 Growth rate, feed efficiency and feed consumption of White Pekin ducklings* (mixed sexes)

		Feed conversion		Feed per bird	
		Weight of feed per unit of liveweight			
Age in weeks	Average weight	For period	To date	For period	To date
	kg	kg	kg	kg	kg
1	0·19	1·14	1·14	0·21	0·21
2	0·60	1·82	1·61	0·75	0·97
3	1·11	2·50	2·02	1·28	2·25
4	1·68	2·73	2·26	1·55	3·79
5	2·18	3·22	2·48	1·62	5·42
6	2·58	4·44	2·78	1·75	7·17
7	2·95	5·16	3·08	1·92	9·09
8	3·29	6·01	3·38	2·02	11·11
9	3·57	7·82	3·73	2·20	13·31

*Source: New York State Poultry Industry Co-ordinated Effort.

involved, including the provision of adequate feed and water trough space, adequate floor or land area per bird and the avoidance of disease.

The inter-relationships in the duck industry have some bearing on these factors, thus, production, which is on an all-the-year-round basis, is normally organised in one of three ways:

- The complete process of production is carried out as one enterprise, ie breeding, hatching, rearing, fattening and sometimes processing and packing.
- The purchase of day-old ducklings from breeders—growing and finishing them as one enterprise.
- The separation of the growing stage into two parts with specialised rearers for the first three to four weeks and separate fatteners for finishing ie for the final three to four weeks.

The question of disease has to some extent always influenced production methods and where different establishments are responsible for each stage, there is often better control. This applies in particular to diseases of the Salmonella group and to Virus Hepatitis, the control of the latter being much better now that an improved vaccine is available. But as with any enterprise engaged in 52 week/year production, management and hygiene must be first-class.

Egg-laying varieties
When rearing future layers or breeders the aim is even growth and fitness to withstand the strain of a high rate of egg production. Checks in growth must be avoided if ducklings are to be reared economically.

Hatching usually takes place in April or early May, but to meet a demand for laying stock replacements or to obtain the maximum number of progeny from specially selected parents, it is sometimes necessary to prolong the season.

Stocking densities
Ducks grow so quickly that it is easy for them to become overcrowded. The fact that table ducks quadruple their weight within four weeks gives some indication of their accommodation requirements. Overcrowding should be avoided as this leads to uneven and poor growth, and vice.

Table 4 shows suggested stocking densities for growing ducklings.

Table 4 Recommended stocking densities for growing ducklings

Age (days)	Wire floor Duckling per m²	Solid floor Duckling per m²
1–10	50 (0·02m²/duckling)	36 (0·03m²/duckling)
10–21	25 (0·04m²/duckling)	18 (0·06m²/duckling)
21–49	8 (0·13m²/duckling)	6 (0·18m²/duckling)

Sun verandas, which provide additional space may be attached to the front of each compartment and one measuring $3·5 \times 1·5$ m is adequate for 100 ducklings up to four weeks of age.

At the three to four week stage fattening ducklings are sometimes moved to outside grass runs in which case the stocking density is normally about 2500 ducklings per ha. This figure is only a rough guide and if there is ample long grass a higher stocking density of up to 5000/ha could be used, the idea being to prevent the colouring in the skin of the bird at killing time from being too deep a yellow.

Bill trimming
Overcrowding, lack of water, sporadic feeding, use of pellets, and dry weather have all been suggested as possible causes of feather pulling. In many instances outbreaks are probably due to a combination of factors including the temperament of the strain of duck involved. Unfortunately not only is the appearance spoilt, but the affected ducks may suffer pain, and are more easily hurt during catching. If such is the case, it may be necessary to trim the bill, but in practice if done at around one week of age, only about 1 mm should be removed, the aim being to remove the shaped bill rim only, in order to prevent gripping of feathers or down. An electric bill-trimmer should be used for taking off this rim and searing it at the same time to prevent bleeding. When trimming is done at two weeks of age slightly more needs to be removed since the rim is wider but if carried out correctly no bleeding occurs, and it need only be done once. The operation should only be carried out by skilled personnel or under their supervision.

Housing adult stock

General requirements
Although the number of eggs laid depends on many factors, including the breed and strain, good management contributes considerably to the achievement of optimum production.

Flocks always include a few nervous ducks and if these are frightened by predators or the sudden appearance of strangers, bright lights or shadows at night, they transmit this nervousness to the others. It is desirable to site houses in positions that minimise disturbance.

It is essential that ducks should always have access to fresh drinking water. It is not advisable to allow mature ducks to have constant access to feed as they tend to put on unwanted fat, it is better to have hoppers of a type that can be shut during the day and opened at night. In this way wild birds are denied access to the feed if the house is open, and ducks can feed quite happily in the darks

Water for swimming is not a necessity for adult ducks and, during a cold. winter, breeding and laying stock are probably better off without it—swimming in cold water can impair fertility.

When adopting an extensive system the pens should be sufficiently large and well sited to ensure that some good grass is available and that the area does not become a muddy waste. Provided that there is some dry ground, there is no objection to ducks having access to marshy areas. Confinement to limited areas of marshy land is not recommended and may lead to the ducks getting out of condition and suffering from infections of the eyes and nostrils.

In the Dutch system ducks are kept in rows of small narrow pens, eg, 5·5 × 1·8 m each containing ten breeders or layers. In this system no attempt is made to retain grass or other herbage in the pens. The ground has to be well drained, preferably sandy, and slope gently. Shelter is provided at the top of the pens and running water along the foot. Where single duck pens are used, the width is reduced to about 0·5 m. The whole area should be enclosed in a high wire netting fence as protection against predators.

Free range
Where it is possible to disperse flocks, or when only one flock is kept, the free range system has advantages in that a certain amount of feeding stuffs expenditure may be saved and penning costs avoided. It is usual to allow approximately 0·5 ha to each 100 ducks. The system may be suitable on a general farm where it is not wished to add to labour by feeding separate pens, or if there is marshy ground unsuitable for other stock. In foraging for feed, ducks can be of use in clearing ground of slugs and snails responsible for harbouring liver fluke which affects cattle and sheep.

Types of housing
Although ducks can live entirely in the open without any form of housing, layers and breeders should be adequately housed if eggs are required through the winter months. Ducks need protection from keen winds and lay better if they have a dry bed on which to sleep. As ducks lay about 95 per cent of their eggs during the night, many of these would be either lost or taken by wild birds and animals if they were allowed to lay outside. Furthermore egg collection would be less efficient.

A pen of about eight breeders needs only a small lean-to type house, say $2·4 \times 1·2 \times 0·9$ m high at the back and 1·2 m high at the front. This gives 0·36 m²/bird. About 0·3 m² of floor space per bird should be allowed for flocks of 50 or more.

Houses, which need not be elaborate, should be sited on dry ground with windows and doors away from the prevailing winds. The roof should be provided with gutters and if the water is not to be collected, down spouts should lead to proper soak-aways. In addition, unless the ground is free-draining it is as well to surround each house with a stone-filled trench to reduce the chances of waterlogging and subsequent puddling by the ducks. Similarly the house entrance for the ducks which should be wide, should lead on to a well-drained area. A simple shelter is illustrated in Fig. 2.

Wire-floored houses have not become popular although there are obvious advantages, notably no litter is needed, there is no contact between the birds and their droppings and cleaning out need not be frequent. Twelve gauge (2·6 mm) welded wire of 25 mm mesh is sufficiently strong and is also wide enough for the droppings to pass through. If such floors are fitted approximately 300 mm above sloping concrete, cleaning is more easily carried out. This type of floor has been made to work where the ducks are allowed outside during the day and it is felt that they could be kept intensively in this way if sufficient ventilation is provided to remove the excessive amounts of ammonia from the droppings.

Solid floors are best made of concrete which is easier to clean and disinfect.

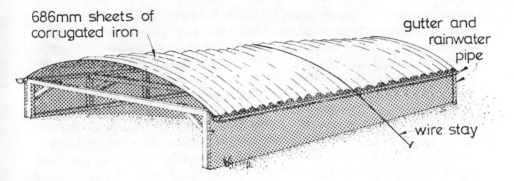

686mm sheets of
corrugated iron

gutter and
rainwater
pipe

wire stay

Perspective View

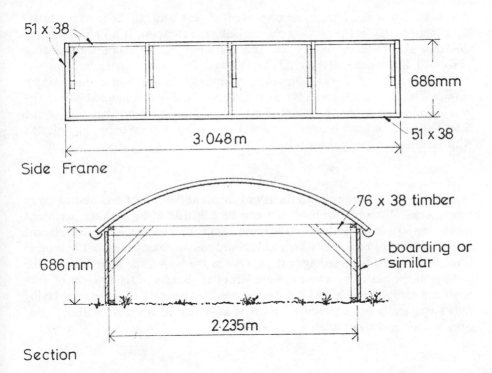

51 x 38

686mm

3·048 m

51 x 38

Side Frame

76 x 38 timber

686 mm

boarding or
similar

2·235m

Section

Fig. 2 Shelter for 100 ducks

To keep the building rat-proof, wire netting should be embedded 300–400 mm below ground. (See Technical Bulletin No 12*.)

To prevent the birds from being frightened by passing traffic it is inadvisable to have windows at floor level—they should be placed as high as possible. Too much light is not to be recommended and some houses have no windows at all

*Technical Bulletin No. 12 *Proofing of Buildings against Rats and and Mice.*

25

but are ventilated by means of baffled inlets. Plenty of air is needed as ducks dislike a warm stuffy atmosphere. Low roofs and stuffy summer sleeping quarters are regarded as contributory causes of early moulting and broodiness. If they are housed at night in a stuffy atmosphere, it is noticeable that immediately they are let out on a frosty morning they temporarily collapse, whereas birds released from a well ventilated house are not so affected. These symptoms are most likely due to the presence of ammonia in the house and show the necessity of having a good ventilation system. With small flocks natural ventilation works satisfactorily and the ideal is to have a long narrow house.

For large flocks housed under one roof a well insulated house with controlled ventilation is a necessity (Plate IV). The advantages of good intensive housing are: economy of labour, the better utilisation of the feed provided—with no feed loss to wild birds and the unlikelihood of a frozen drinking system.

Litter materials

Peat moss, wood shavings, straw or pulverised pine bark can be used for litter, but chopped straw is the popular choice, being the cheapest. It is important that the straw should be clean, dry and free from mould, especially, for breeding birds. All litter materials should be renewed frequently particularly in the sleeping area. If the litter is damp there is always a danger from moulds which may penetrate the shell and adversely affect egg quality and hatchability in the case of breeding flocks. Frequent checks should be made on the state of the litter to prevent it from becoming too wet or too dry or from becoming infested with parasites or harmful organisms.

Nest boxes

Nest boxes should be provided for laying ducks at the rate of one nest to every three ducks. A simple form of nest can be constructed by making partitions measuring 30 × 35 cm and mounting these 33 cm apart using a 15 cm wide board running along the back and a 5 cm wide board running along the front at ground level. Such a nest is placed against the wall of the house, the floor forming the bottom of the nest. Front and top are left open. Blocks of six or eight of such nests are easily portable and can be removed for cleaning. The nests of laying ducks frequently become soiled and it is advisable to clean them thoroughly once a week and renew the nest material.

General management—adult stock

Breeders

Breeding stock should be mated at least one month before hatching eggs are required. At this time the change to a breeding diet should also be made. With table strains a mating ratio of one male to five or six ducks is usual with perhaps even seven in springtime. This is usually increased to one male to six or seven ducks for laying strains.

26

Flock size

Currently flock sizes of about 200 ducks are common, although some authorities still consider that groups of 40–50 laying ducks provide the best compromise between the better performance associated with very small numbers and the saving in labour and equipment possible with very large flocks. With large flocks economies are achieved, particularly in feeding, as large hoppers facilitate bulk delivery direct from the lorries of the feed supplier. A possible though unlikely disadvantage is the risk of losses occurring if the ducks become excited. While much has been said in the past about the excitability and nervousness of ducks, it has been found in practice that although they may appear to be frightened and make a lot of noise when disturbed, production is not usually affected even by such operations as routine vaccination or wing banding. Nevertheless it is important to carry out these procedures in an orderly manner avoiding unnecessary distress.

Hatching egg production

There have been two approaches to the problem of getting a uniform supply of ducklings throughout the year. As with all stock, performance declines as the length of the production period increases, thus at least two flocks are needed by any producer wishing to maintain fairly even production.

The first system allows the ducks to produce eggs for as long as possible—that is until the output of ducklings becomes near to being uneconomic. In practice this point may be reached (in a normal flock) at any time from about 18 up to 30 or more weeks, and depends on the date of hatch (or the date on which production started) as well as on other factors including the characteristics of the stock itself. Production is terminated by a natural or enforced moult involving an unproductive period of 10–12 weeks. Normally two cycles of production are achieved before a flock is culled.

The second system is more rigid and involves imposing a fairly regular pattern of alternating 18–20 week production periods with forced moult/resting periods of about eight to ten weeks. Breeders expect three such cycles for a breeding flock. The advantages claimed for the system are that it facilitates effective production planning and that average production, fertility and hatchability levels are higher.

In the winter months fertility may be improved by subjecting the males to a 17-hour day by the use of artificial light for two weeks before the females are housed.

Moulting

Ducks tend to moult according to their hatching date. For instance, spring-reared birds will probably do so during the early part of the following year, whilst those produced in the autumn, during July and August. Moulting may be induced by ceasing artificial lighting, giving no feed for 24 hours, but maintaining access to water. From the second day an allowance of 140 g per bird of

27

whole grain should be given. It is advisable to start feeding 170 g of a breeders diet three weeks before bringing the ducks into lay. During winter and where runs are in poor condition, a holding ration (see Table 3) may be considered more suitable than the whole grain feeding mentioned above.

Broodiness

Ducks are not so prone to broodiness as hens and if kept away from comfortable sitting places they soon get over it. Broody ducks can become vicious and, if handled, hiss and raise their feathers in protest.

Feeding

Young stock

A starter diet compounded especially for ducklings should be used (or as an alternative, a broiler chick starter). The feed, which should be given as soon as the ducklings are put into the brooder may be either crumbs or 3 mm pellets; crumbs are not as satisfactory as pellets since they are inclined to be more dusty—the dust sticks to their bills and fouls the drinking water. Wet mash is now seldom used.

Apart from the first few feeds when such receptacles as shallow trays or biscuit tin lids (provided the edges are not sharp) may be used to hold feed, troughs can quite easily be improvised from galvanised guttering. Well designed feed troughs or hoppers help to reduce waste (Fig. 3).

As the ducklings grow they should be given deeper troughs which hold more feed. Allow approximately 0·5 m of trough space per 100 birds from nought to

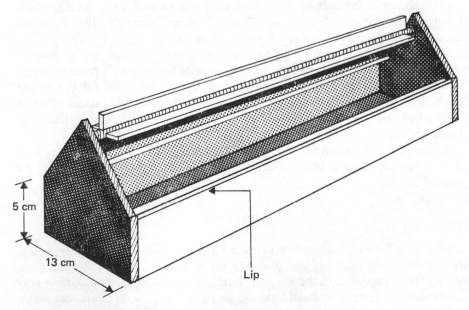

Fig. 3 Smallflock pellet feeding trough—Note anti-waste lip

three weeks of age. Both feed and water troughs must in the early stages, be placed near to the brooders so that the ducklings can find them easily.

After the brooding stage it is now common practice to feed pellets. On large units bulk delivery of feed into large hoppers or where convenient, into bulk bins for subsequent automatic feeding results in cheaper feed and a lowering of labour costs.

Fattening

Fattening should be regarded as a continuous process from day-old to killing. As there is a marked fall in feed conversion as the duckling increases in age (see Table 4), it is essential that they are brought to killing weight in the shortest possible time. The object nowadays is to produce a duck of around 3·2 kg liveweight at 46–49 days. If the ducks are fattened outside, it takes an extra week to attain the same weight in inclement weather. It is common practice to feed a starter ration for the first three weeks and then to use a grower/finisher ration. Alternatively, after three weeks of age a grower ration can be used for 2½ weeks followed by a finisher ration which is lower in protein and thus cheaper.

Future breeders

At eight weeks of age ducks intended for future breeding are given a holding diet designed to be adequate for development but not for the laying down of fat. Provided range is available and there is ample room to forage a pellet feed in the morning and a grain feed at night will keep such stock in a healthy condition. It is advisable to feed future breeders up to no more than 75 per cent of appetite.

Adult stock

In a free range situation the feed hoppers should be so constructed that they can be closed down to keep out wild birds. Opened up at dusk, they allow the ducks to feed during the night. For pellet feeding 2·4 m of trough space is adequate for 400 ducks.

Water

Clean water in suitable containers is important. Ducks are fond of water but should not be allowed to get too wet, particularly when very young. Drinkers should not be so deep or large that the ducklings can immerse themselves but the water should be sufficiently deep to allow the immersion of their heads. If they cannot do this, their eyes seem to get scaly and crusty and, in extreme cases, blindness may follow. They also like to clean their bills periodically and to wash them clear of feed. For the first week or so small metal founts are useful and their size should be increased as the ducks grow. Automatic watering (Fig. 4) can be used from day-old provided the containers are designed to prevent the ducks paddling in them. There are a number on the market, but before buying it is advisable to enquire whether they are suitable because some that are satisfactory for chickens may become clogged with feed when used for ducklings.

In the case of egg production stock, it is worth encouraging the young ducklings to exercise during the growing stage by placing the feed and water containers some distance apart. The habit of eating and drinking alternatively ensures that they are constantly on the move.

If the ducklings have left the brooder house at an early age (at about three weeks) the larger sized top-filling founts will be suitable for a further two weeks.

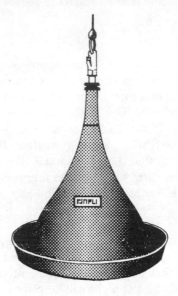

Plastic round drinker

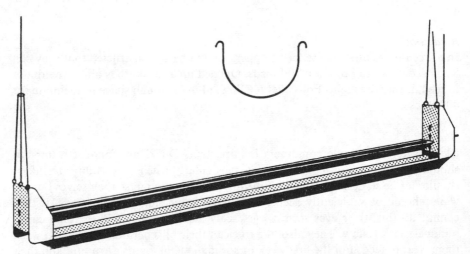

Galvanised drinker (with cross-section)

Fig. 4 Automatic watering

After this, larger water containers can be used. Ducklings do not need to be able to bathe.

Drinkers should be scrubbed daily to prevent accumulation of mash which quickly turns sour. It is sound management where applicable, to place all drinkers on a wire or slatted platform to reduce the amount of water that finds its way into the litter.

Outside, where water is laid on to the field, troughs can be fitted with ball valves to ensure a constant supply. If mains water is not available tanks filled periodically can be connected to the troughs by flexible tubing.

Production, processing and marketing

Marketing regulations
In many countries there is a determined effort to improve the standard of hygiene in poultry processing. In some areas this has resulted in new legislation which replaces that already existing. While most large scale processors in Europe are covered by legislation based on Directive 71/118 EEC and its amendments, there are many smaller businesses which will need to comply with existing national rules. Thus in the UK, large processors will need to study carefully the requirements of the Poultry Meat (Hygiene) Regulations 1976 and smaller ones the Food Hygiene (General) Regulations 1970. A draft EEC Regulation on Marketing Standards for Poultry meat is also under discussion. It contains proposed specific quality requirements covering grading, temperature limits, packaging, labelling etc. at various stages of marketing. It would apply to the marketing of ducks and geese as well as to other species of poultry.

In general terms these regulations require that poultry should only be processed in buildings suitable for the purpose, that processing carried out in these buildings is done hygienically and that the buildings are maintained to a high hygienic standard. The majority of poultry meat will also be subject to meat inspection.

It is important for prospective producer-processors to obtain copies of the relevant legislation and seek the advice of the official responsible for its implementation. For further information see:

Slaughter of Poultry Act 1967.
Slaughter of Poultry Act Extension Order 1978.
Slaughter of Poultry (Human Conditions) Regulations 1971.
Food Hygiene (General) Regulations 1970 SI No 1172.
Poultry Meat (Hygiene) Regulations 1976 SI No 1209.

Production data and costings

Table duckling

Profit is dominated by market price, which in turn is a reflection of demand and supply for the size and type of bird being produced. It is essential that the marketing outlets should be properly arranged before production gets under way. Failure to observe this rule may well result in disaster.

Most table duck production today is in the form of frozen oven-ready ducks although some are still produced as 'New York Dressed'.

Like other sections of the livestock industry duck producers have at intervals had to contend with an over-supplied market, but the larger producers have partially overcome this by installing their own cold storage facilities. By selling retail the smaller producers have an advantage that is not open to the large scale producer.

Production costs vary considerably, being influenced mainly by feed conversion efficiency, scale and system of production, disease incidence and mortality and by the type or strain of duck. Efficient management depends on the availability of relevant and reliable information on these and some other production factors.

Because the collection of data tends to be laborious and costly, it is well worth examining the whole enterprise carefully to determine which records are necessary and the degree of precision required in the recording. An insistence on unnecessarily high levels of accuracy increases cost. Furthermore when such records are combined with less accurate ones a false sense of precision may be created.

Table 5 gives figures from a recent costing (1977) exercise on a fully intensive unit and shows that margins are tight, a reduction of 5p/kg or a widening of the conversion ratio by 0·27 would nearly cancel out the profit.

Table 5

6000 per crop	= 39 000 per house per annum
Age at killing	= 49 days
Average liveweight	= 3·22 kg
Average OR weight	= 2·36 kg
Feed consumed	= 8·79 kg
Feed conversion ratio	= 2·73:1
Price received per duck—88p/kg	= 208p
Food cost—£125/t	= 110p
Day-old cost	= 25p
Fuel, electricity and water	= 6p
Other variable costs	= 4p
Cost of processing, marketing, boxes etc.	
11p/kg OR weight	= 26p
Total gross costs	= 171p
Labour (£2500)	= 6·4p
Building/equipment depreciation	
(cost £56/m²—7·5 duck places = £7·50/duck place)	= 11·6p
(At 6·5 crops pa = £1·16/duck—at 10%)	
Other fixed costs	= 3p
Total costs	192p
Margin	= 16p

The essentials of a profitable enterprise are summarised thus:

● Good housing and management with efficient temperature control and ventilation.

32

- A good strain of ducks, well managed to give good conversion ratios.
- The use of suitable rations and avoidance of waste.
- Efficient marketing.
- The keeping of accurate records.

Although each enterprise varies appreciably, the figures for intensively kept ducklings shown in Table 5 (page 32), provide a starting point against which actual results can be compared. It should be emphasised that the system of housing (particularly as this affects feed wastage), the quality of the feed, the type of duck, disease incidence and season all may have some effect on the results obtained, so the figures shown should be treated only as a general performance guide. Where income is lower or costs higher than those shown, this provides a basis for investigation. Special situations may enable a producer to reduce some costs below those indicated—the starting point for achieving this is a sound record keeping system.

Factors often neglected include the overhead costs attributable to the enterprise. Because overheads can be calculated more accurately on an annual basis and because there are seasonal variations in both running costs and prices, the comparison of one year's results with another usually gives the best guide to overall efficiency. Crop by crop records provide valuable information to assist in the making of both husbandry and management decisions. In this respect liveweight at marketing, feed consumption and mortality are the main efficiency indicators. It should be noted that if production is not continuous, the length of the rearing and fattening periods is not important, provided that feed consumption, carcase quality and weight are not adversely affected.

Preparation for market

Killing

As with chickens and turkeys there is little difference between the weight of the sexes during the first few weeks of growth. However, by killing time the males are usually 227 g or so heavier than the females. Apart from weight, the stage at which ducks are killed has an important effect on the quality and appearance of the carcase.

With modern equipment and especially when wet plucking is carried out, the stage of feather growth in ducks is not now quite so important as it used to be. Even so, the best results are only obtained when birds are fully feathered, well finished and in good condition. Killing should start when the feathers begin to fall from the neck and breast and the flight feathers are 70–90 mm long. This stage is called 'first feather'. A few fatteners keep some of their birds on to what is termed 'second feather' which means that they have already moulted once and there has been a second growth of feathers. This normally takes a further five to six weeks. The resulting 12–13 weeks-old bird is about 25 per cent heavier, but to achieve this additional weight a lower feed conversion efficiency has to be accepted.

Before killing, the birds should be starved for at least six hours so that their intestines will be empty. When marketing un-eviscerated, the carcases keep

33

better and eviscerating is made easier. Although starvation for much over six hours results in some loss in carcase weight, in practice this is unavoidable where substantial numbers are involved. Water should remain available for as long as possible.

Killing can be either by dislocation of the neck or by stunning and 'sticking'. In both cases the method should be learnt by demonstration. Attention is drawn to the 'Slaughter of Poultry Act' and it is essential that its requirements are observed.

Dislocation

Dislocation of the neck is a satisfactory method of killing provided it is properly done. As a duck's neck is rather long, this is not always easy. Where only a small number of ducks are involved, killing can be made easier with the help of a broom handle. This is placed on the floor across the neck of the duck at the point just behind the head. The person who is killing stands on the handle astride the bird which is pulled quickly upwards so that dislocation is rapid. It is important that there should be complete severance of the spinal cord leaving a good gap at the point of dislocation otherwise the body blood will not drain completely. Failure to drain properly leaves excess blood in the carcase resulting in a poor appearance due to a reddish tinge of the flesh.

Sticking

This method is necessary if the birds are to be sold as 'oven-ready'. The birds should first be stunned, which may be achieved with the aid of an electric stunning knife or, on a large scale, by their passing through a stunning machine. Then the brain is pierced via the roof of the palate and the jugular vein severed. Before plucking the birds must be bled out and for this purpose specially shaped cones, often mounted on a circular stand are normally used (Fig. 5).

Plucking

Hand plucking is tedious and only appropriate for small numbers. It is best carried out as soon after killing as possible. For moderate numbers or where the ducks are to be sold uneviscerated dry plucking combined with wax finishing is the method of choice.

Dry plucking machine

The birds are stripped of feathers by machine, finishing being carried out by hand. Feathers still command a good price and dry ones are more valuable than wet. Plucking should start immediately the bird is killed, and the tail and large wing feathers taken out first by hand and kept separately. The machine operation takes one to two minutes. The remaining stubs must be removed by hand but it is better to delay this until the carcases have cooled for not only will the stubs then come out more easily but there will be less likelihood of pieces of skin coming away with them.

The down that clings to the flesh is difficult to remove. If only a small number of carcases is involved, singeing is a satisfactory method. A small quantity of

34

methylated spirits is placed in a flat vessel and ignited—the resulting clear flame does not cause any taint. For large numbers of carcases wax finishing is effective.

Wax finishing
Following dry or wet plucking, this method of removing any remaining feathers and down is an important and widely used alternative to singeing. It is appropriate when large numbers are involved. Hot paraffin wax is held in thermostatically controlled tanks at a temperature of 60°C. After immersion in the wax for about five seconds the carcases are removed and either sprayed with cold

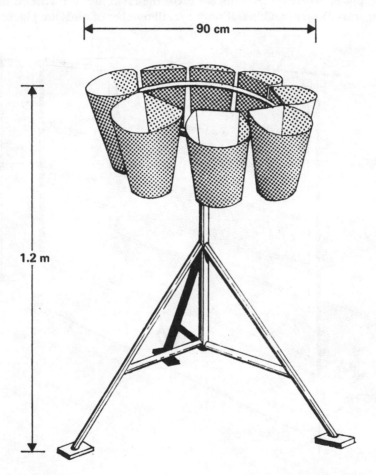

Fig. 5 Draining rack

water or immersed in a cold water tank. The hardened wax, which may be stripped off by hand or by using a rubber-fingered drum plucking machine, can be reclaimed and used again after heating to 99°C and straining to remove the feathers. It should be pointed out that an offence may be committed under the Food and Drugs Act (1955) if at the point of sale any wax is found adhering to the duck.

*Marketing uneviscerated**

As soon as plucking is finished, the wings should be folded back and the legs and bill scrubbed to remove dirt. The improved appearance makes the operation well worthwhile. The legs should then be twisted back so that the inside of the webs of the feet are against the bird's back. Any faeces that are found in the vent must be squeezed out. The duck should then be cooled rapidly to an internal temperature of 4°C. As it is necessary to get rid of the body heat as soon as possible, specially designed cooling racks are used for holding the carcases (Fig. 6). These racks are sometimes on wheels for convenient movement from place to place. Where cold rooms are used, the racks are just wheeled in, thus avoiding unnecessary handling. If only a small number of birds are plucked they

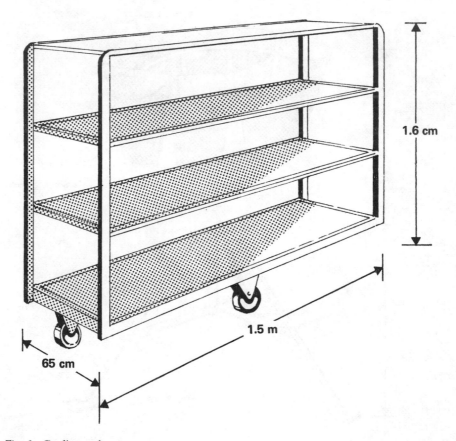

Fig. 6 Cooling rack

can be laid flat on the breasts with weights over their backs. This will press them down and give them a broader breast which looks more attractive. If the ducks are to maintain their appearance and quality it is essential for them to be properly cooled before they are packed in boxes for distribution.

*See page 31.

Wet plucking

Most ducks are now sold eviscerated and frozen. Some of the large fatteners have deep freeze facilities and eviscerating lines on their farms and can carry out the whole production processes from brooding to packing.

The birds are first electrically stunned and then pass a revolving knife at the beginning of a conveyor line. This cuts into the blood vessels of the neck and the blood drains into a trough as the ducks pass along the line. After passing through a scald tank at 60°C, progression is via a rubber-fingered plucking machine, through a hot wax dip, then a cold dip to set the wax followed by removal of the wax and down (Plate VIII). The ducks are finally conveyed into the next section. Following evisceration they are cooled in either slush ice or a spin chiller. After draining, the carcases are weighed and placed in plastic bags. The giblets are usually wrapped in plastic film and put inside the body cavity.

Freezing

Before storage and/or transport at freezer temperatures, carcases have to be frozen. There are several methods of freezing including blast freezing in which a stream of fast moving air at −40°C is blown over the carcases, brine freezing in which the carcases are immersed in a brine solution maintained at −18°C, and less commonly through the use of propylene glycol. The first method is widely used but the second gives a much whiter carcase.

Packing

Non-returnable cardboard boxes are the standard means of packing and because of rough treatment it is essential that they should be strong and well made. A box to hold four ducks weighing 2·2 kg oven-ready will need to measure 53·6 × 28·9 × 11·1 cm (BSI Recommendation). The cost of boxing is about 6·5p per kg of oven-ready birds.

To obtain uniformity the ducks must be graded for quality and size. Second quality birds should be disposed of separately and some fatteners sell them either unbranded or under a separate brand name.

Marketing

Ducks are not usually marketed alive for they do not travel well and lose weight in transit. In whatever way the birds are to be marketed and however large or small the consignment may be, arrangements should be made well in advance and marketing properly organised.

Although there are various demands for ducklings, such as from wholesalers, dealers, retailers and caterers, the duck trade is unlike that of other table poultry, being more specialised with less comprehensive distribution. Most ducks are sold to the catering trade where the demand is tending to move towards the smaller bird which yields adequate half-duckling portions. Producers are responding by adopting smaller strains and by killing their ducks at an earlier age.

Sales to the housewife are limited because of some consumer resistance. Apart from an apparent lack of knowledge on ways in which ducks may be cooked, the duck suffers a handicap because of its fairly high cost in relation to the amount of meat on its carcase. This is illustrated in Table 6 which compares the 2·7 kg duck with other table birds. The data are meant only as a guide as yields depend upon sex, strain, age of birds and particularly on processing techniques.

In spite of the handicap of an unfavourable yield of edible meat, much could be done to encourage consumers to consider duck more favourably. In particular the excellent flavour of the flesh might be stressed. Additionally there is scope in some areas to make duck more readily available than at present. This, in time would help to increase the interest of the housewife for a commodity that has been rather neglected. More could also be done to improve the attractiveness of the oven-ready bird by using colourful packaging. Suitably worded labels stuck on containers would help to engender interest. The labelling of food is governed at present by the Food and Drugs Act 1955, particularly Sections 1 and 6, by the Labelling of Food Regulations 1970 (as amended); and by the Weights and Measures Act 1963 and subsequent regulations. The sale of food is also governed by Sections 2 and 8 of the Food and Drugs Act 1955. These rules are enforced by the County Councils and London Borough Councils, who should be approached for advice or with complaints. All of Section 8 and some aspects of Section 2 of the Food and Drugs Act, however, are enforced by District Councils.

The label should describe the bird in a way which is accurate and not misleading as to its nature, substance or quality. If the bird has been processed in any way the nature of the processing should be made clear. The label should carry a list of ingredients (if any) in descending order of proportion by weight, and the name and address of the packer or labeller. The net weight, in imperial and metric terms, may also be required. The inclusion of cooking instructions is an additional way to improve the image of the table duck.

Table 6 A comparison of processing and cooking losses in different types of poultry

		Ducks 2·7 kg	Geese 5·0 kg	Turkeys 3·6 kg	Broilers 1·8 kg
Starved liveweight					
As per cent of starved liveweight	Bled and plucked weight	82	90	90	87
	Eviscerated weight (including giblets	73	72	78	75
	Cooking loss (Roasting)	37	35	31	22
	Yield of edible cooked meat	25	29	34	27
Yield of edible cooked meat as per cent of eviscerated weight		35	40	44	37

Marketing duck eggs
The importance of duck eggs for human consumption has declined strikingly since the immediate post-war years when duck eggs accounted for between two and three per cent of all eating eggs produced and about four per cent of those

passing through egg packing stations. Although there is some prejudice against duck eggs, their food value is very similar to that of hens' eggs.

Whether intended for human consumption or for setting in an incubator, careful attention should be paid to handling and hygiene. Nest boxes should be re-littered frequently with good, clean straw or shavings to ensure that eggs are as clean as possible when collected. Even when nest boxes are provided, some eggs are laid in other parts of the house and in consequence tend to get dirty very quickly. Each day, as soon as the birds are let out, the eggs should be collected into clean containers, the dirty ones being kept separate. It is important that receptacles should be easy to wash and disinfect, and plastic coated wire baskets are favoured.

The eggs should be taken immediately to a cool room and those that require cleaning should be washed as soon as possible. After rinsing off the worst of the dirt using warm water from a hose or tap, each basket should be placed in a bucket or tank containing warm water and a recognised cleaning agent, at a temperature of 46°–49°C. After the basket has been agitated for about half a minute, it should be removed and the eggs thoroughly rinsed in water at the same temperature. Washing water in the tank should be changed frequently and certainly after each two or three baskets full. It is important to maintain the temperature at the suggested level to avoid a tendency for harmful organisms on the surface of the shell to be drawn in through the pores by contraction of the egg contents, a hazard that results from washing in cold or cool water.

After allowing to drain and dry in the basket, eggs should be packed in clean fillers or, if to be sold retail, candled and graded before packing.

By-products
Although there seems to be an increasing demand for duck livers (for inclusion in pâté) and a limited sale of duck feet to the Far East, probably the main saleable by-products of the duck and goose industries in this country are feathers and manure.

Feathers
The amount of feathers on a duck or a goose depends on its age, weight, and whether it is in first or second feather, but as a guide five ducks produce approximately 0·5 kg of feathers.

The analysis of chicken feathers is as follows and while that of duck feathers is not available there is some similarity:

	Per cent
Protein	73·15
Water	21·6
Fat	1·01
Ash	1·11

The protein contains an essential amino acid called cystine which is rich in sulphur. Duck feathers are too valuable to be sold as manure which is the fate of a large proportion of both chicken and turkey feathers. At plucking time the quills and stiffer tail feathers are thrown aside and kept separate as it is the feathers from the body proper that are in demand, particularly those from the breast which are the finest and softest.

Some years ago the income from feathers was considered to pay for the cost of plucking but when feather value decreased and costs escalated this was no longer the case. Now (1978) the dry duck feather value has risen to over £1 per kg for poorer quality mixed feathers, and up to about £3·30–£3·90 per kg for really good quality feather with down included (the last two prices are for feathers obtained from dry plucking machine or hand plucking. The wet material (dried) from modern processing would not be likely to come up to this sort of quality).

The use of feathers in the domestic and commercial world seems to be increasing. They have long been used for pillows, quilts and cushions, and they are also valuable in the making of flying suits or where light insulation against intense cold is required.

Recently, feathers have been used for decorations of many kinds, mainly in the production of artificial flowers. An appreciable proportion are duck and goose feathers, but particularly the latter. They lend themselves to bleaching, dyeing and painting, and the results after careful and skilled handling, can be very attractive. The wing feathers of the goose have long been used for making shuttlecocks and in the feathering of arrows used in archery.

Manure
Analyses from different manures from poultry is given in Table 7. Allowing for differences in moisture content there is little difference in the manurial value of duck and hen manure.

Table 7 A comparison of manurial value of droppings for some classes of poultry

	Percentage				Number of samples
	Moisture	Nitrogen	P_2O_5	K_2O	
Duck droppings	32–60	0·8–3·2	1·4–2·3	0·6–2·2	2
Duck slurry	95	0·5–0·6	0·5–0·6	0·1	2
Duck—straw litter (2 months in open)	6	0·4	1·0	0·6	1
Hen battery droppings (average)	73	1·5	1·1	0·6	73
Hen battery slurry (average)	92	0·6	0·5	0·2	59
Broiler litter (average)	28	2·4	2·2	1·4	129
Goose (fresh)	75	0·6	0·6	0·8	1

The wetness of duck manure makes it difficult to handle when unmixed with litter. Accumulations of wet manure or slurry may be removed from sumps or storage tanks by means of vacuum pumps or augers. In conjunction with large mobile containers large quantities may be removed in a matter of minutes and then distributed on the land.

Most of the nitrogen in poultry manure is soluble and readily available to the plant and it is inadvisable to store it for long. If storage is unavoidable it should be under cover to prevent leaching. The drier the material can be kept, the less likely it is to give off obnoxious smells.

Geese

Breeds

WITHIN living memory the types and breeds of fowl, ducks and turkeys have increased in number, but the few useful breeds of geese have remained much the same for hundreds of years. The reproductive performance of the main classes of poultry have been greatly improved, but commercial geese seem to have deteriorated in reproductive ability over the past 50 years. Most of those seen on farms today can be said to be of the 'barn-door' type and can hardly be related to any breed. Frequently they go under the guise of *Embden/Toulouse* crosses, a description that may bear little relation to their actual ancestry.

Geese vary considerably in size and quality, some being quite large and of good quality, ganders weighing up to 9 kg at nine months of age and geese up to 7·75 kg. Others are small and poor in quality with the ganders weighing no more than 4·5–6·5 kg. If a particular breed is required, great care should be taken when buying new stock.

The *Common* goose may vary from mainly grey to mainly white. Buff and light salty-blue varieties are occasionally found. Although these colour varieties can appear from matings of the common goose, true breeding varieties have been produced. Thus we have the *English-Grey*, the *English-White* and the *English-Grey-Back*. The *Grey-Back* has also been called *Saddleback* and *Pomerian* as it is very common in parts of Germany.

English-grey, English-white, English-grey-back

Under these names can be classed the various colours of geese found in this country and known as *Embden × Tolouse*. The white is, perhaps, the one most worthy of improvement but there are good strains to be found in all three.

Weights vary greatly from strain to strain, but a weight of 7·75–9·0 kg would be representative for the gander and 6·5–7·2 kg for the goose.

Egg production also varies but may be said to be between 30 and 40 eggs in a season, laid in two or three clutches. In a few strains up to 80 eggs are sometimes produced, usually by very hardy geese that are generally good sitters and mothers, and are the best types for the general farm.

Embden

The *Embden* goose (Plate III) appears to have been imported from Germany in the early part of the 19th century. In 1815, both male and female were referred to as being white and of 'very uncommon size', but in spite of this, they were very slow to become popular. By 1872, weights of well over 13·5 kg had been obtained and in 1929 the British Standard was 13·5–15·5 kg for the gander and 9·0–10·0 kg for the goose.

Toulouse

The *Toulouse* (Plate III) is a grey goose imported from southern France by the Earl of Derby in about 1840. They were then called *Mediterranean*, *Pyrenean* or *Toulouse*, but the last-named is now the only one used. They seem to have been much larger than the *common British* goose, but not so large as the *Embden*, the Standard weight being 12·75–13·5 kg for the gander and 9·0–10·0 kg for the goose.

Although as pure breds both the *Toulouse* and the *Embden* may be looked upon largely as exhibition types of limited economic value, crosses in the past with the *common British* goose greatly increased the body.

Roman

The *Roman* (Plate II) is a medium-sized, white goose; a better layer than the *Common* goose, but not so good as the *Chinese*. Being one of the most economic of our pure-breds it is very useful for present-day requirements when a very large, fat goose is not needed.

In spite of claims to Roman origin, the first reports of this goose in the United Kingdom and the United States do not appear until the early part of the 20th century. One authority suggests that the *Roman* is very suitable for killing when in first full feather and should be kept small. But so far 'broiler' goslings have not become popular although such young birds are very good to eat and are one of the cheapest forms of meat to produce.

Adult weights have been put at 4·5–6·5 kg for the male and 3·5–4·5 kg for the females, but the lower weights would bring them into the *Chinese* class, which seems a little too small. The suggested 6·8 kg for the adult gander and 6 kg for the adult goose, seems more appropriate.

There is a *Crested Roman* goose bred in America but although crested geese often appear as sports in English geese, no crested breed has been produced in this country.

Many pure strains of this breed are autosexing (see page 47) from their down colouring but only for the first two or three weeks.

Buff

Early writers do not mention *buff* geese but there is little doubt that *buff* sports from the *common grey* goose have appeared from time to time for many years.

The colour may be due to crosses with the *Fawn Chinese*. In 1928, Sir Rhys Llewellyn obtained some *buff* geese from a Breconshire hill farm, bred them and called them *Brecon buff* geese by which name they are usually called in this country. They were recognised by the British Poultry Club in 1934.

Buff geese are medium-sized, good table-quality birds and fair layers, combining attractive looks and usefulness while making less noise than the *Chinese*. Their colour is similar in marking to the *Toulouse*, except those parts that are grey in the *Toulouse* are a medium to light buff. The adult gander weighs 8·5 kg and the goose 7·25 kg.

A *Buff-Back* is also bred, similar to the *Grey-Back* except in colour.

Chinese

The *Chinese* goose is said to have ranged all over China, Siberia and North India and has been known as the *Knob, Spanish, Polish, Muscovy, Siberian, Guinea* and *Swan* goose! It has a swan-like neck and is thought to have been bred from the wild goose of China and not from the *Grey-Lag*, although it interbreeds with the *common* goose, the *Grey-Lag* and, according to Cuvier, with the *White-Fronted* goose.

It seems to have been known in Britain in the 18th century and used to be a good layer, although today many strains are little better than the *common* goose. However, *Chinese* geese have been known to lay in November and produce records of up to 140 eggs per bird in a year.

There are two colours; Fawn and White. In the Fawn, the body colour is a fawny-brown with white edging to the feathers on the back and wings. The front of the breast and neck are light brown. The top of the head and back of the neck are dark brown. In crosses with the *Grey* goose this dark neck strip is transmuted to dark grey. The neck stripe, but not the brown colour would appear to be dominant. The bill and knob are black or dark green, the latter being at the base of the bill, and much larger in the male than the female. The legs are dark orange. *White Chinese* have orange bills, knobs and legs.

In the pure state, *Chinese* geese can be sexed at about six to eight weeks because of the gander's larger knob. This is a very useful characteristic and it seems a pity that in this country it has almost been bred out in one strain, making it just as difficult to sex as the *common* goose.

The *Chinese* is very small weighing little more than 5·5 kg for the adult male and 4·5 kg for the adult female. As a table bird, it is no larger than a large duck, and as it also has darker flesh and its dense down makes plucking, difficult, it is not a popular table variety with the trade. They are ornamental, very good 'watch dogs' and can be killed at any time from eight weeks old.

Breeding methods

There is no reason to doubt that the selection methods used to improve other species of poultry would not also be effective for geese. Unfortunately little research has been carried out and few breeders have attempted to improve

44

the performance of geese economic characters. Exhibition types of some breeds have been developed considerably, but the objectives have often run counter to utility requirements so the resulting stocks are of limited value to the commercial breeder.

Undoubtedly the main factors limiting the introduction of effective selection schemes for geese have been the low average size of flocks coupled with poor reproductive performance and late maturity. With small numbers of birds intense selection for body size or reproductive characters would be expected, after a few generations, to result in a high rate of inbreeding. This in turn would tend to have the effect of depressing reproductive performance even further, so that such a breeder might find that any initial progress had been cancelled out. With the occasional development of flocks running into several hundred birds and with breeding sets being numbered in scores, rather than twos and threes, a very real opportunity exists for substantial progress to be made.

Although the peculiarities of the species must be accommodated in any breeding programme, the principles of selection outlined here serve as a basis.

Selection from the best families for egg production, fertility, hatchability and in some cases viability may well prove worthwhile. In selecting for better conformation, birds with prominent keels should be avoided. Ideally the keel bone should be slightly recessed, giving a 'dimple breast'. Additionally the breast should be broad and long.

To speed up improvement breeders are increasingly employing cross-breeding methods. Although by no means a new development, such crosses as the simple *Embden* × *Toulouse* seem to give rise to progeny which benefit from hybrid vigour. Many of the goslings imported each year from Denmark are *Embden/Roman* crosses. The *Roman* geese give the breeders better egg production than would pure *Embdens* and the resulting goslings grow rapidly to an acceptable size.

Any crossing programme should be backed up by proper recording and selection procedures, and reference may be made to the main section on breeding on page 42.

Apart from the *Chinese* and *Roman* which are much more productive, the average goose lays two clutches of 15–18 eggs each season. Under natural conditions lay commences about the end of February, but earlier production can be induced by good feeding and possibly by additional (artificial) light.

With good grazing, swimming water is not essential for fertile eggs to be produced, although results tend to be better when it is available. If not available a trough large enough for the geese to immerse their heads and necks should be provided.

In the wild state, geese pair and mate for life. Under domestication geese also mate for life given the chance, but a gander will mate with several geese. The older breeders used to run five or six geese with a gander; today this ratio is regarded as satisfactory for the *Chinese* breed. With the *English* and *Roman* breeds four or five females to each male is enough. For the larger breeds, particularly when of exhibition type it is usual to use ratios of one gander to two or three geese.

Making up sets

Geese do not take to one another readily as do fowls, turkeys and ducks. They must be well used to each other before they will breed. All the geese in a set (a breeding pen of geese) must be friendly, and the gander must have been with them for some time before they will mate. Six weeks is about the shortest time that they should be together before fertile eggs can be expected, and the longer the period, the better the results. This is possibly why second-year geese frequently give better results than first-year birds. It is often said that the first egg of a goose is always infertile. This is not correct but the idea may have arisen because the birds have not been together long enough. For good results sets should be made up by Christmas or earlier for the next season's breeding, and good ones should not be broken up so long as they remain good breeders.

Geese are productive for many years. It has been known for a 25-year-old goose to give 100 per cent hatchability of all eggs. There are also records of geese breeding for 70 or more years although perhaps ten years for a goose and four to five for a gander may be taken as an average useful life.

Replacements

Should a gander die or become infertile his geese will take to another gander after about six weeks or more. It is difficult to add another goose to a set if one should die or more are required. In this eventuality the following procedure may be adopted. First remove the gander out of sight and sound. Then if possible place the remaining geese of the set in another field or house before introducing the replacement(s). If they drift apart they must be confined to a small run until they are feeding happily. Provided this comes about, which will take from four to six weeks or more, the gander may be reintroduced. The temptation to return the gander too soon should be resisted as he may well drive the new bird(s) away, even if accepted by the original geese.

Mating

Several sets can run in one field without wire netting pens, provided there is a separate house for each set and that they are mated before they are run together. Initially the sets should be confined in small temporary pens some distance from each other.

When they seem to be mated, each set should be put in its own house and left there for a day. After that they can all be let out and will keep in their sets. It is best to feed each set near to its own house.

Should a mixed flock of geese and ganders be put randomly together, results can be expected to be poor, since some dominant ganders collect a large number of geese whose eggs they cannot hope to fertilise, while bullied ganders are left with the odd goose or none at all.

Where fertility is low, or non-existent in single pens of breeding birds, a check should be made that the supposed gander is really a male and has not been mis-sexed and, likewise, where production is low and some 'geese' appear not to be laying, they should be sexed again, since it is possible that if pens are made up when birds are immature, mis-sexed birds can get into the breeding flocks or pens.

Sex differentiation

There are three main methods by which the sex of geese can be determined, these are:

- On the basis of down and plumage colour in the case of breeds in which the sexes naturally differ, particularly the *Roman*. Also in the case of those crosses which can be made to produce colour differences. These are dealt with under the headings of auto-sexing and sex-linked crosses respectively.
- On the basis of gross appearance, other than colour, and on behaviour.
- By examination of anatomical differences in the region of the vent.

This examination may be carried out while goslings are no more than a few days old or again when the birds are mature (Plate IX). In between it is possible but very difficult.

Plumage colour

Auto-sexing

Auto-sexing geese seems to have been known for many years. Most old accounts suggest that the '*Common* gander is invariably white' and that when the *Embden* was first introduced into this country breeders were surprised that both sexes were white. Normally the *common* goose was grey.

The auto-sexing characteristics seems never to have been highly regarded. With the spread of the *Embden* and *Toulouse* breeds the auto-sexing strains of the *common goose* have virtually disappeared.

The *Pilgrim* goose which is now very uncommon is a pure auto-sexing breed with different feather colouring at all ages. Some strains of *Embden* and *Roman* show colour sexing in the first few weeks only, the males being paler grey than the females. In these cases genetic factors controlling the expression of colour eliminate the difference before the birds are actually feathered. If vent-sexing is to be avoided later on, the sexes should be marked by toe 'punching' or wing banding while small enough to colour sex.

There are two wild species which exhibit sex-linked colour differences, these are *Chloëphaga hybrida hybrida* or the *Rock* or *Kelp* goose, and *Chloëphaga picta picta* or *Upland* goose, both from the Weddell Sea area—there is no evidence that these were ever domesticated or crossed with domestic geese.

Sex-linked crosses

The two pairs of sex-linked genes influencing plumage colour which have been identified in geese can both be utilised in making sex-linked crosses. Examples include crosses between some strains of *White Chinese* males and *Embden* females, when the female progeny will be generally darker than the male; and crosses between *Embden* males and *Toulouse, Brown Chinese* or *African* females. In this case the adult males will be light grey in colour and the females white.

In the reciprocal cross, *Toulouse, Brown Chinese* or *African* males mated to *Embden* females, the adult male progeny will have lighter grey plumage than the female.

Appearance and behaviour

Except in the cases of auto-sexing geese, sex-linked matings and the *Chinese* and *African* breeds, where the larger knob on the head of the male can be seen at about eight weeks of age, it is not possible to tell the sex of geese until they are at least nine months old. Even then experienced observation is required.

The gander is usually slightly larger than the goose, has a longer thicker neck and a larger and more bull-like head. The normal voice of the gander is shrill and that of the goose of appreciably lower pitch. The alarm note in both sexes is much the same. When approached, especially with a dog, the gander or ganders will come to the outside of the flock although both sexes lower their heads and hiss.

Vent-sexing (at day-old)

An experienced goose stockman makes few mistakes in sexing geese by appearance, but the only sure way is by examination of the vent. This is best done at one day old and the goslings marked (by toe punch, leg band or wing band) accordingly. If missed during the first few days of life it is easier to wait until the birds are mature.

The goslings should be taken in the left hand, the head down and the breast to the palm of the hand, The back of the middle joint of the index finger of the right hand should be placed just below the tail which should be grasped between the index finger and the thumb and pulled back and down. At the same time the vent should be opened with the thumb and index finger of the left hand. In the gander the male organ appears as a small protuberance about 3 mm long.

Sexing fully grown birds

Each bird should be held between the knees with its head out behind and the back uppermost. The tail should be grasped and forced back with one hand while the other hand opens the vent. With a gander, this may need a little force, but the vent of the goose usually opens easily. The inner surface of the vent of the goose is wrinkled and loose, the colour a dark pink to light red.

The inner surface of the vent of the gander is smooth and a very light pink; the male organ, which is quite large, is almost white in colour. The colour of the inside of the vent must be noted as soon as it is opened because if the bird is a gander and some time is taken in exposing the male organ, or fully opening the vent, there will be some inflamation, and the colour difference disappears.

Another method is to have an assistant to hold the bird on its back on a table

48

Brooding on wire

Fattening on wire

PLATE I

Roman gander

Pekin duck

PLATE II

Khaki Campbell duck

Utility Aylesbury

PLATE III

Embden goose

Toulouse gander

PLATE IV

Duck breeding houses showing bulk bin to automatic feeders and egg room

Vaccinating breeders before and between lays for duck virus hepatitis and Newcastle Disease

PLATE V

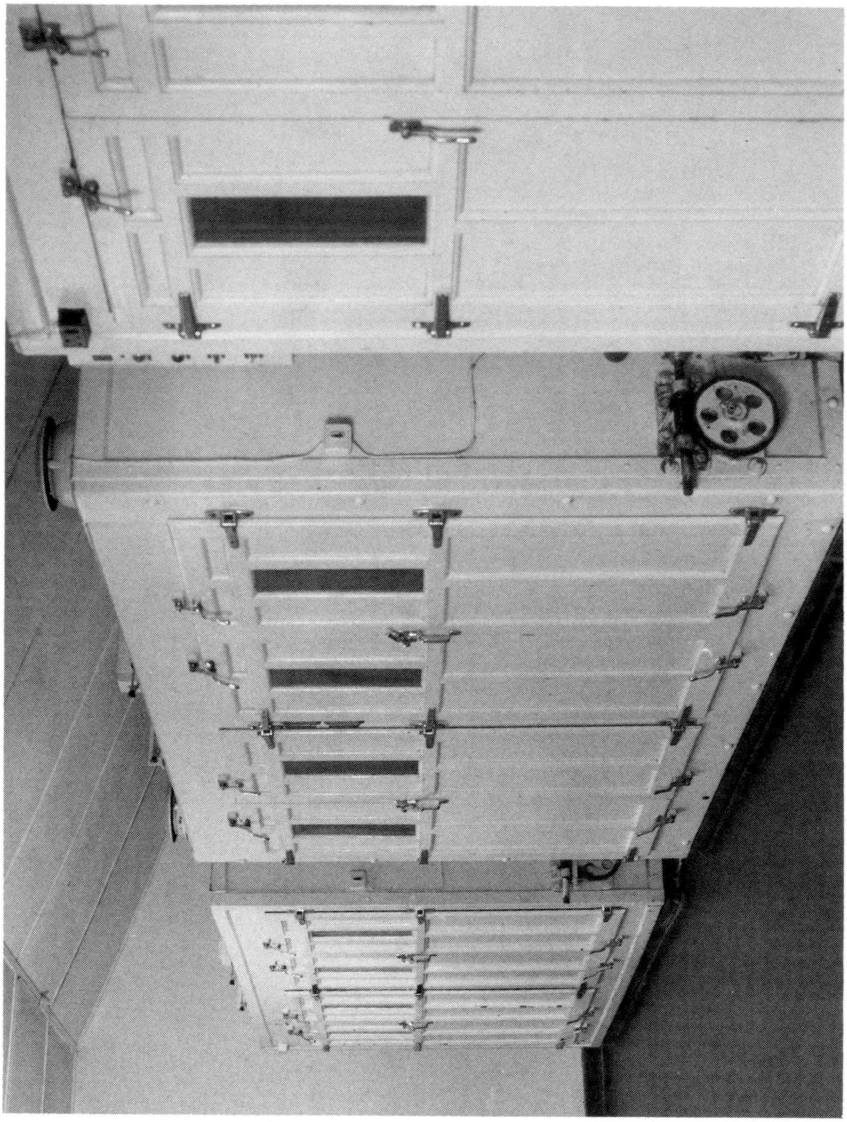

Incubator setter room with hatcher room beyond

PLATE VI

Egg holding, showing heater/cooler and the day's eggs sanitised, marked and partly trayed

PLATE VII

Floor brooding – Most of drinkers from first day are on wire-floored ramp at rear

PLATE VIII

Field fattening

Modern brooding and fattening wire-floored house – pressurised ventilation with fibre glass ceiling

PLATE IX

Close-up of Plate ix, showing below floor outlets and opened fail-safe panel
Waxed ducks entering cold water tank for setting

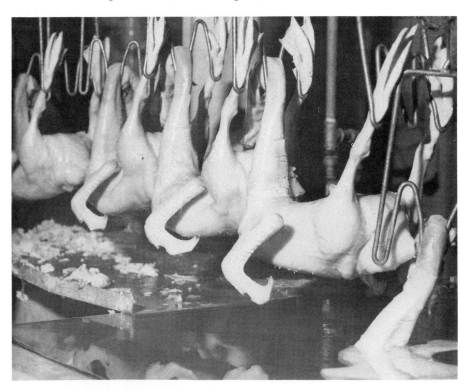

PLATE X

Wax jacket being removed for reclaiming

PLATE XI

A gander:
Position of hands for
opening vent. The sex
organ has been exposed;
note the pale colour
compared with the outer
skin and inner surface of the
vent of a goose illustrated
below

A goose:
Position of hands for
opening vent. Wings
should be held up by the
arms and not allowed to
hang loose (see above);
note darker inside of the
vent of the goose

PLATE XII

or on the ground. Both hands should be pressed on either side of the vent to expose the inner surface.

Once identified, leg banding or wing tabbing should be used to ensure that the birds can be subsequently recognised.

Incubation

Geese eggs take from 29–32 days to hatch and incubation may be natural or artificial. Geese are usually good sitters and mothers, but, if eggs are to be hatched a number of large boxes or 'hides' should be placed near the goose houses but some distance from each other. There should be at least one box for each goose, and straw and a china egg should be placed inside some time before eggs are expected. This helps to ensure that each bird has her own nest. If more than one goose lays in the same nest there will be trouble when one of them goes broody and the hatch could be spoilt.

A goose should be shut on her nest so that the others do not worry her but she must be let off to feed once a day. If she does not come off of her own free will she should be taken off. Geese have been known to starve themselves almost to death when sitting.

At hatching the goose should be shut on her nest until the hatch is over or the other geese may interfere with her. When all the goslings are ready to leave the nest they can be let out with their mother and, provided the grass is very short, may be allowed to run with the other birds. The gander may help to look after the young goslings; in fact he sometimes makes a good 'mother'.

Hatching under hens

On many farms, eggs making up the first clutch are collected each day and set under hens. When a goose goes broody, she should be shut off her nest for a few days until 'cured' and she should lay again in two or three weeks. This is another reason why a nest for each goose is desirable. If several geese lay in one nest, the broody must be shut up in a cage or crate for about three to four days. During this time she must be fed and watered, and the crate must be within sight and sound of other geese. The goose may then be allowed to sit on her second clutch which would normally be the last of the season; but *Chinese* and other good layers may lay three to four clutches, if encouraged to do so.

Broody hens are set in the usual way. It is generally suggested that the base of the nest should be made up of earth or a grass sod upside down because this will hold the moisture. It is also a good foundation for the nest which should be made of straw or hay.

After the hen has been sitting on the new nest for several days, the goose eggs may be placed under her. A good hen takes four to six eggs according to size. She should be let out to feed once a day at which time a little warm water should be run into the grass sod or soil under the hay or straw. This provides most of the moisture needed until the last two or three days when the eggs may also be sprinkled lightly with warm water.

In addition each day the eggs should be turned over completely leaving the narrow ends towards the centre of the nest. The hen does shuffle the eggs a little, but this is ineffective with such large ones in ensuring the complete movement of the embryo within the egg.

Artificial incubation

(For conversion of °C to °F see Appendix 2)

It is not yet known how to achieve really successful incubation of goose eggs in incubators, and much conflicting advice is given. For example, as the normal temperature of the goose is slightly higher than that of the hen, it is difficult to see why it is suggested that the incubation temperature should be run one degree lower for geese than for hen eggs. This idea possibly arose from using old type hot-air incubator, where it is not possible to alter the height of the thermometer. The bulb of the thermometer is, therefore, about a quarter-way down the large goose egg instead of just at the top, as with the hen egg. In such a machine, the temperature should be lower, but in hot-air, natural-draught machines where the thermometer can be adjusted, it is better to raise the thermometer so that the bottom of the bulb is just at the height of the top of the average-sized egg. The temperature should then be run as for hen eggs, at a constant 39·5°C for 29 to 32 days.

Eggs should be turned twice a day at 12-hourly intervals. All moisture devices supplied with the machine should be kept filled throughout the incubation period. In hot-water machines, such as the Hearson, no extra moisture is needed and it is advisable to air the eggs after turning for about five minutes in the second week, ten minutes in the third and 15 minutes from then to the 27th day. In hot-air machines no airing is needed; but one felt should be removed on the 10th day and the second on the 18th day. It is advisable with goose eggs, which require slower air movement than hen eggs, to use a third fairly thin felt or thick hessian until the last turning when the eggs start to 'pip'. It should then be removed.

The inside of hot-air machines may be sprayed with water at about 45°C with a mist-type sprayer each time the eggs are turned; but it is best not to spray or sprinkle the eggs themselves.

Humidity

Most operators overdo moisture and since incubators vary, a careful watch should be kept. Goslings incubated under too low a humidity are rather small and often have bits of shell sticking to them; those hatched under too much humidity are rather large and the down does not fluff out well. A note should be made of those that pip the shell and then die. If the shell is just broken and the gosling dies with its bill sealed with albumen, humidity has almost certainly been too high. If the bird bills the shell some way round the egg and then dies humidity will probably have been too low.

Ventilation

Poor ventilation in the machine or incubator house affects the eggs in a similar way to excess humidity and this point should be watched. Poor ventilation may result in high mortality from about the 20th day onwards.

Cabinet incubators

Few breeders use cabinet machines; but the 'paddle' type has given good results. With some machines every other setting tray must be moved or the goose eggs cannot be inserted, but sometimes they can be laid flat and every tray utilised. These machines should be used as for hen eggs, but in some makes better results are obtained if the temperature is kept slightly higher than for hen eggs, while in others it may require to be a little lower to give the best results. This can only be ascertained by trial and error.

Testing

Eggs should be tested weekly during incubation starting at five or six days when the faint spider-like embryo can be clearly seen with a good lamp—through to the 26th or 27th day just before pipping starts. The reason for the more frequent testing than is done with hen eggs, is so that 'bangers' can be removed in addition to infertiles and ordinary dead germs. 'Bangers' is a loose term used for 'wet rots' or mouldy eggs, which are likely to explode either in the incubators or while being tested outside. They can spread mould spores, various bacterial organisms and other undesirable material around the hatchery. These are not uncommon in goose eggs which are frequently laid in damp places. Fertility should be consistently over 80 per cent for older birds but is very substantially lower in first season breeders. In fact some farmers feel such eggs are hardly worth setting and prefer to use them for eating. Similarly hatchability of eggs from young birds is usually poor.

Eggs stored for up to a week hatch reasonably well in incubators. They will do as well kept up to ten days under hens and up to a fortnight under the geese themselves provided they have been laid in a dry clean nest with plenty of material for the goose to cover them.

In the case of goose eggs no good estimation of the rate of evaporation from the egg is possible by looking at the air cell with the aid of a candling lamp. There is too much individual variation for this to be done successfully, and it may be that incorrect decisions would be taken on such evidence.

If slow-hatching goslings are helped out of the shell, they should be given plenty of time to dry off and 'harden' before being removed from the incubator when many such youngsters will rear quite well.

Machine capacity

One goose egg takes up the space of three to four hen eggs, and as the capacity of most incubators is given in terms of hen eggs, a good idea of the goose egg capacity can be obtained by dividing the hen-egg capacity by four. In some cabinet machines it is necessary to remove alternate trays from the setters and hatchers, thus making it necessary to divide hen-egg capacity by eight.

The special incubators made for turkey eggs are more satisfactory for goose eggs as there is more room between the trays.

Management

Brooding and rearing

Under natural conditions, goslings reared by the goose remain with the flock until the following breeding season when the old birds drive the younger ones away. With traditional commercially reared geese this does not happen because the young birds are usually sold off by Christmas at the latest. There is no harm in allowing the young birds to remain with the old ones until towards the end of September, when they can be taken away and fed on a finisher feed for two or three weeks to 'harden' the flesh before killing and freezing. If they are to be eaten as 'Michaelmas' or 'Green' geese they can be taken straight from the adults and from grass for killing. It is now considered quite uneconomic to feed geese on expensive rations throughout the autumn to kill fresh for Christmas. Some autumn grass may be lush but lacks the feeding value of earlier season's grass so that the producer may think his goslings are getting on well but is disappointed with the weight and condition they have lost when left to fend for themselves after the end of September. With the above two alternatives ruled out, the best method left is to feed well for two or three weeks in October to finish the birds, killing and freezing them early in the autumn.

Marking
It may be difficult to differentiate between early hatched goslings and old geese by killing time and much handling is saved by toe-marking the goslings at day-old using a different mark for male and female ones if they have been sexed at hatching. A different mark can also be used for different years. A simple slit can be made with a sharp knife in the web between two toes. This grows into a 'V' shaped mark. Up to 16 such marks can be made by single or combination cuts using only one in each web. If brooded artificially goslings may be leg or wing-banded before they go outside to graze, so that later in the summer, different ages and sexes can be recognised more easily.

Natural brooding
The goose or hen automatically broods the goslings. Hens in fact remain with them long after they need brooding. There is no harm in allowing this but the hen may be taken away when they are three weeks old.

Until they get their first feathers it is important to prevent young goslings from running in long wet grass or being out in heavy or continuous rain, otherwise they may get chilled and die. The mother goose usually looks after them in wet conditions but a hen may not. With artificially reared goslings (up to three or four weeks of age) having access outside, provision must be made to drive

52

them inside during heavy rain. Goslings can swim when only a day old and come to no harm.

Artificial brooding

Generally, good chicken brooders are suitable for geese, but like ducklings, goslings make rather a mess of cloth curtains or canopies. Brooders needing these are not advised, nor are those with steep ramps such as the warm floor type. They can be reared on either wire or solid floors. About 15–20 goslings, according to size, may be placed in one 100-chick brooder (maker's capacity).

If oil heating is used the pyramid type is possibly the best but electric brooders are more suitable and infra-red heaters are almost ideal. Dull and bright emitter infra-red lamps are equally good but the drinkers should be placed well away from them as goslings are apt to splash the water about and should a lamp be splashed with cold water it may be broken.

The same heat is required as for chickens (38°C) on the floor of the brooder and about 150 mm away from the heater. With infra-red heaters a mercury thermometer will not give a true reading, but red and specially blue spirit ones give a near enough reading for practical purposes.

A good guide to the height of infra-red lamps is to note the position of the birds when asleep at night. If they will not sleep directly under them, but form a circle around the centre leaving an open space beneath, then all is well. If they crowd right under the lamp, it is hung too high.

During the daytime goslings go right under an infra-red lamp but normally remain there only a short time. Should they tend to huddle, the lamp should be lowered.

After the first week goslings need little heat but they do need some until they are about three weeks old after which it is normally unnecessary provided the litter is kept dry and clean. Goslings need cleaning out much more often than chickens. Their droppings are much wetter so that the litter soon becomes sodden if not changed. Damp litter may lead to poor growth.

Rearing

As previously mentioned goslings should be allowed to run on short grass at the earliest possible age. With hen or artificial rearing the birds should be restricted to a small pen or run for the first two weeks. After this they can find their way about quite well and may be given virtually unrestricted range.

Almost any kind of poultry house with a solid floor is suitable as a brooder house up to eight weeks old. After this time a rough shelter will suffice so long as the floor can be kept dry. If allowed to do as they like, goslings of eight weeks old or more would probably choose to sleep in the open air or on a pond if they had access to one. This would be all right in sheltered districts if there are no foxes, but it is safer to provide some housing.

If they have outgrown their portable brooder house, geese may be housed in a shed, stable or other buildings at night and driven to a pasture for the day. If given a small feed most of them will come home on their own at shutting-up time.

Feeding

Geese are natural grazers and under traditional husbandry systems profitability is dependent upon access to ample short-growing herbage. It is quite wrong to think they thrive on long, coarse grass. Young geese may starve to death on such grass and older birds eat little but the seeds. At the same time, they will eat many weeds and herbs which other animals avoid such as buttercups, both herbage and roots. They also graze creeping thistle while the plants are small.

Breeders

During the winter months breeding stock should be maintained in a store condition that is on a restricted feeding regime. If good grazing is available a light grain feed each evening may be all that is necessary to maintain them in breeding fitness. If grazing is not available the birds may be fed oats, good silage, pulped mangels and leafy hay during the holding period. In these circumstances grain should be fed night and morning and consist of no more than can be cleared up in ten minutes.

Breeders' pellets should be fed for at least four weeks before hatching eggs are required, initially on a restricted basis and with some grain. When laying commences the pellets should be fed *ad lib* with a small amount of grain, and grazing or green feed as available. Breeders must never be overfed, but the diet should be of good quality. The eggs from overfed geese tend to be less fertile and may show poorer hatchability.

The vitamin supplement should contain A, D_3, B_2, B_{12}, and Niacin, and because the ration is advised to be fed as a balancer, a complete mix with pantothenic acid, folic acid, E and K in addition would be a useful insurance. Either the goose diet in Table 8 or the duck diet in Table 2 may be used for breeding geese.

Gosling starter

Day-old goslings may be started on 3 mm pellets followed by 5 mm ones from two weeks of age. A complete feed may be fed *ad lib* and grower size insoluble grit sprinkled on the feed twice weekly. Mash may be fed but feed conversion is likely to be less efficient than when the feed is pelleted.

If such a feed cannot be obtained, or home mixed, goslings do quite well on duck starter crumbs or pellets, preferably in conjunction with good grazing. Goslings, given the chance, start grazing before they are 24 hours old, and if on ample high quality close-growing herbage do well with little additional feed. When such pasture is not available and when they are reared under hens or by artificial means, supplementary feeding is needed.

With hen rearing, the coop and run should be on short grass and the run moved several times a day. Small feeds of goose or duck starter for the goslings and grain for the hen are all that is needed in the way of feed for the first two weeks. After that time grain alone is often sufficient, provided the grass is good and less than 100 mm long.

Although goslings have traditionally been considered as not taking kindly to intensive conditions, there is increasing interest in devising systems for this purpose. One of the difficulties often encountered is the strong instinct of goslings to nibble. In the absence of grass, turves or green feed such as cabbages, they start nibbling each other's down, which leads to bare backs and heads and more serious vices. Bill trimming may help if there is a severe problem (see page 23). In some cases strips of tough cloth hung up can alleviate the problem by providing something for the goslings to 'play with'.

Under any intensive system a complete diet must be provided. This can be in the form of pellets or crumbs, or a balancer supplementing regular daily supplies of freshly cut green feed.

Goslings grow very rapidly and reach 3·5–5·5 kg in 12 weeks, according to breed. After this they grow more slowly and may not put on more than a further 1·8–3·5 kg. *Chinese* will add 1·0–1·5 kg before reaching adult weight.

Duck starter as in Table 2 may be fed to goslings as an alternative to that in Table 8.

Growing and rearing stages

From two or three weeks of age goslings may be fed on the growers diet given in Table 8 or, as an alternative, on the growers diet for ducks in Table 2. On range it may be fed on a free-choice system with whole grain, the mixed feed being pelleted. Under intensive conditions faster weight gains are achieved, but the advantage of feed saving through grazing is lost. For intensively housed geese the growers diet should be fed alone until the geese are nine weeks of age, offering grain and grower feed on a free choice basis after that stage. Pellets give better results than mash and hen-size insoluble grit should be provided *ad lib*. For the last two weeks they may be given the duck finisher diet in Table 2. This is particularly desirable if the birds are to be processed and frozen, since a complete ration preferably away from grass is thought to give a harder flesh more suitable for freezing purposes.

Table 8   Goose diets (kg/t)

	Starter	Grower	Breeder
Wheat (coarse ground)	300	350	250
Barley (finely ground)	200	300	200
Maize (freshly ground)	300	200	300
Dried grass	50	—	—
Meat and bone meal	20	30	60
Fish meal	50	30	60
Soya bean meal	60	70	80
Limestone (flour or granules)	10	10	40
Dicalcium phosphate	5	5	5
Salt	5	5	5
Vit/Min supplement	12	12	12
Calculated analysis			
Crude protein %	16	15·6	18
Calcium %	1·09	0·98	2·57
Energy k cal/kg	2765	2788	2733

These diets are designed to be fed in conjunction with good grass (and where desired) a small feed of grain in the case of the growers and breeders.

Stocking rates on grass

Stocking rates for geese on grass can vary from 20–60/ha according to the quality of the sward. Benefit can be derived from alternate grazing and resting, to allow pastures periods of recovery. During rearing on range satisfactory results have been reported for flocks stocked as heavily as 750/ha from four weeks to killing at 10–12 weeks. *Ad lib* feed must be provided during this time.

Processing and marketing

Killing

Care should be taken in handling birds as they are easily bruised when fat which detracts from market value. Feed should be withheld 12 hours before killing. Geese are usually killed by dislocating their necks. A description of suitable methods is given on pages 33 and 34. It is essential that the techniques involved should be properly demonstrated and newcomers to the job must be properly supervised.

Plucking

Although the plucking of geese is not easy, the methods practised are similar to those used for other classes of poultry. Removing the feathers by hand is tedious, so if large numbers have to be done a dry plucking machine can speed up the operation. Goose feathers are a valuable by-product and those from the tail and wings should be kept separate from those of the body. It is the latter, particularly if they are white, which make the most money.

At present dry goose body feathers complete with down make up to £6·50/kg while wet plucked feathers may only fetch about £1/kg after drying.

Dry plucking undoubtedly produces the best carcases but scalding eases the job. The carcases are immersed in water at a temperature of 50°C for a few minutes or until the feathers pull away freely. American sources suggest adding a little of an approved detergent to the water to act as a wetting agent. Where this method is adopted the carcases must be kept moist during evisceration and until packed. Wet plucking is unsuitable if the carcases are to be marketed uneviscerated. As with ducks the method of choice for a medium or small scale operation would be dry plucking coupled with wax finishing. The plucking and evisceration lines used by the duck fatteners can, with little modification be used for small and medium sized geese.

Evisceration and trussing

Details are given in Appendix 1.

Packing

After evisceration, geese can be wrapped in the same way as other table poultry and made to look attractive. Although a large number of geese are produced for selling unfrozen at Michaelmas and Christmas, increasing quantities are deep frozen.

The average goose (5·4–6·4 kg liveweight) loses about ten per cent of its liveweight in feathers and blood and 20 per cent in drawing. Of the 70 per cent trussed, uncooked weight, about nine per cent will be bone. Table 9 shows the growth pattern of traditionally grown table geese up to seven months of age.

Table 9   Liveweight (kg) of medium sized geese at various ages

At hatching	0·09–0·11
4 weeks old	0·9–1·6
8 „ „	2·5–3·1
12 „ „	3·4–4·3
16 „ „	3·8–5·0
20 „ „	4·3–5·4
24 „ „	4·8–5·9
28 „ „	5·9–7·2

Marketing

In goose production the greatest profit is made by those who hatch, rear and sell goslings at two to eight weeks of age.

There has been a gradual decline in the production of table geese over the past few years. Causes for the decline in popularity appear to be the poor quality of many of those produced and the high percentage of fat associated with the goose. Both improved feeding and the greater latitude in time of killing and processing that is now possible due to deep freezing and cold storage leads to better quality. Greater care over marketing, including packing, grading and publicity could also help to improve the image of the table goose.

Most geese are sold in the pre-Christmas period when, in some years, prices become very attractive. Recently demand has been good and prices have ranged from 120p to 150p per kg plucked and even over £2 per kg oven-ready. On the other hand, at times prices drop dramatically and producers putting birds on to the market at the 'wrong' time have been unable to sell at an economic price.

Table geese may be sold alive to packers or slaughterers, or they may be killed and plucked on the farm. To maximise returns, and often profit, sales should be made direct to consumers and retailers. For this trade it is usually essential to pack and dress the birds. It is always wise for producers to confirm orders and agree prices well in advance. Hoteliers are not normally interested in geese as they claim that they are expensive.

Goose liver

A by-product industry is the preparing of goose livers for making table delicacies. The ancient Egyptians knew that the livers of geese could be increased in size and flavour by excessive feeding, a practice also common in Greece and Italy. The Greeks apparently esteemed the goose primarily for this enlarged liver and were familiar with the cramming of the bird that brings this about. After removal, the liver was soaked in honey and milk to further increase its size and flavour. In the Middle Ages the goose was common in England and the fat goose liver was considered a delicacy, but it was in the mid-18th century that a Strasbourg cook evolved a recipe which is used to this day and known as Pâté de Foie Gras.

Ornamental ducks and geese

Ducks

ORNAMENTAL ducks can be divided into two categories: those which have been bred to their present colour and type; and wildfowl which retain their natural colour and form.

Although many of the domesticated duck breeds qualify by their beauty for the title of 'ornamental', the following breeds together with all wild fowl species are recognised by clubs as those which come under this heading. The wild breeds are fully described in books on ornithology and apart from the fact that the more colourful of these defy a written description, they are so profuse that it would be difficult to describe all that are worth keeping in a collection. There are approximately 240 species and sub-species of wild waterfowl. The following are among the more interesting:

Black Cayuga

The *Black Cayuga* may not properly come under the heading either of a wild fowl or an ornamental. Its ancestry is obscure but if, as many people think, it is a sport from the *Mallard* it may be included on the grounds that it is a direct descendant of a wild breed. As a utility breed its qualities are doubtful but for ornamental purposes its beauty leaves little room for doubt. It appeared in this country in the latter part of the 19th century and is said to have come from Lake Cayuga, New York.

Briefly, the *Black Cayuga* has an intense iridescent beetle-green plumage and black legs as a young bird that turn to a brownish-orange with age. Its eyes are black, a slate-black bill and a black saddle. It is a heavy bird weighing 2·75–3·5 kg with a lively, alert expression, and a 'clean-lined', horizontal body carried clear of the ground.

Black East Indian

The *Black East Indian* (also known as the *Black East Indie*) is also considered by many to be a sport from the *Mallard*. It is generally accepted that the colouring of the Cayuga has been improved by crossing with the *Black East Indian*, which has very intense beetle-green colouring.

In type, the *Black East Indian* is short and broad with a short neck. Carriage

59

is lively, smart and symmetrical and clear of the ground, resembling a small compressed version of the *Cayuga*. The drake of this breed weighs only 0·9 kg the duck 0·5–0·8 kg.

Both breeds lay eggs varying in colour from black, at the commencement of the clutch, to off-white at the end of the clutch.

Rouen

As its name suggests, the *Rouen* is of French origin and noted for its beautiful appearance. It resembles the *Mallard* or wild duck more than any other breed and was imported into this country many years ago. The plumage of both sexes is exceptionally vivid, the bill is a greenish yellow, legs and feet brick-red. The drake weighs about 4·5 kg the duck 4·0 kg.

It is claimed that the *Rouen* has the most distinctive flavour of all breeds. It takes a long time to mature and is not ready for killing before 20 weeks, which makes it uneconomic to keep. Apart from this it is difficult to breed true to type owing to its varied colouring. It lays a green egg.

Decoy, Kooi, Cali, or Mignon

These ducks originated in Europe for exhibition purposes.

There are two varieties of *Decoy*—the *White* and the *Brown* (or *Grey*). The *White* is a pure china white with orange legs, feet and bill. The *Brown* is similar to the *Mallard* in colouring, but the female has darker lacing and the male darker marking. Both from an exhibition and ornamental point of view the *White* variety should be bred as pure white as possible, free from sappy (yellow) feathering. Type in this breed is quite distinctive. The body should be short, compact with close feathering and clear lines. The head is round and puffy with eyes set centrally, bill short, thick and dished. The *Decoy* should be bred as small as possible. Eggs are white to pale green.

Silver Appleyard Bantam

The *Silver Appleyard Bantam* duck was bred by Reginald Appleyard at Ixworth, Suffolk. It is variable in colour. Drakes are beautifully marked in a variety of colours, rose, white, black, grey, lustrous green etc. As its name implies it is a very small bird approximately the size of the *Black East Indian*, or perhaps even smaller. Its type is different from that of other small breeds in that it is rather higher at the shoulders. The line from the tip of the bill to the back of head is straight. Eggs are white to pale green.

Any of the above breeds will lay a clutch of eggs varying in number and, if eggs are not collected, go broody and sit on them. If eggs are collected daily much greater numbers are laid throughout the season.

Many of the wild species of waterfowl, native and non-native, breed well in captivity if kept in suitable surroundings. Most of them are worth keeping in a collection for their beauty of colouring, different habits and voices.

Mandarin and Carolina

Without doubt the *Mandarin* (or *Chinese Love Bird*) and *Carolina* are the most colourful. The former comes from East Asia. In China, at weddings, a pair of these birds is given to the bride by the bridegroom as a token of fidelity. *Mandarins* mate in pairs for life and are very faithful to each other.

Mandarin and *Carolina* females are rather similar in colouring but differ in detail when viewed closely. Both of them are dowdy compared to their males tending to a dark grey with white markings. Both carry a crest.

The males differ considerably. The *Mandarin* has what appears to be 'whiskers'—long pointed feathers from each cheek, and distinctive wing coverts which are lifted to look like sails when the bird is displaying. Both *Mandarin* and *Carolina* males have long crests which hang down to their shoulders and can be lifted at will when the birds are frightened or displaying.

The colouring of the *Carolina* (also *American 'wood'* or *'Summer'* duck) male is not so varied, but the clear markings together with the brightness of existing colours puts him on equal terms with the *Mandarin*. As the bird moves or the sun catches it, the variety of tints and sheens which appear, from what would seem to be single colours must be seen to be believed. Both these birds belong to the tree duck family, nest in the hollow trunks of trees and lay small white eggs.

Various surface feeders and divers

Of the surface feeders the *Widgeon, Chiloe Widgeon, Shoveller* and *Pintail* are well worth keeping as they are all beautifully coloured and marked.

The *Red-Crested Pochard, Rosy-billed Pochard* and *Tufted* are diving duck which afford variety. The *Common Shelduck* (or *'Burrow'* duck) which nests in burrows is attractive and distinctive. A collection would hardly be complete without our common but highly ornamental *Mallard*.

These are but a few varieties of duck which can be kept. They differ in colouring, habits and voice and also cost less to purchase initially than many of the breeds available.

Geese

There is not the variation and brilliance in colouring in domesticated geese compared with domesticated duck breeds, so it might be imagined that the same would be true for wild geese but this is not so and the wild species have great variety of colour, size, habit and calls.

Because of the need for grassland for geese to graze, collections are usually more limited than in the case of wild duck. However one or two pairs of geese are attractive and entertaining and usually become quite tame. Would-be enthusiasts are deterred because geese do not breed well until three years old and the initial cost of some varieties is high. To offset this, geese continue breeding for a number of years and once established are inexpensive to maintain.

Canada, Grey Lag and *Egyptian* (or *'Nile'* goose) are amongst the breeds most commonly kept. They differ widely, the brief descriptions below indicate this variation. Prices for these range from £15 to £20 while the more expensive breeds may go up to £250 per pair. Some breeds have become extinct but thanks to the Wild Fowl Trust and private enthusiasts with collections of different varieties counted in the hundreds, many more breeds of geese and swans in addition to ducks have been preserved.

Canada

This breed has a striking and pleasing appearance. There are several varieties differing slightly in colour and size but are generally as follows: individuals have a black head, except for an inverted V of pure white extending up each cheek behind the eye, and a black neck, the black finishing in a clean line where the neck merges into the shoulders. The rump, tail and wing tips are also black. The breast is grey-brown, the abdomen white and the remainder of the body dark grey-brown, with each feather broadly laced with a lighter shade of grey. Legs and bill are black.

The *Canada* is a large and powerful bird with a long upright neck, fairly short legs, and a long body gently sloping from shoulders to tail which is fairly long and carries on the line of the body. It is a delightful bird but one to be wary of in the breeding season as it guards its nest and eggs zealously. Its call is a deep 'ker-honk'.

Egyptian or 'Nile' goose

The *Egyptian* or '*Nile*' goose is unlike any other variety. In shape it is rather similar to the *Shelduck*, with long legs, small body, round and prominent breast, rather long tail carried low, and upright neck giving it a very active appearance. Its colouring is rich. The head is fawn except for chestnut around the short, coral-pink bill, and a chestnut patch around each eye. There is a little chestnut down the back of the head and an uneven ring of the same colour about half-way down the neck. Apart from a very distinctive blob of chestnut on the breast (the 'target'), breast and under-carriage are vermiculated fawn. Wings are chestnut, with white wingbars, body black and glossy green, undertail pinkish-brown, tail glossy black. Legs and feet are pink. The voice varies in note and resembles a laughing cackle when the birds are excited and 'talking' to each other.

The *Egyptian* is worth keeping for its looks, voice and for the prettily-patterned brown and grey goslings. These birds are extremely vicious in the breeding season when they should be safely penned from other birds and children.

Grey Lag

The *Grey Lag* has head, nape of neck and upper part of back ashen brown. The lower back is blue-grey, each feather laced with lighter colour, wing and tail feathers are leaden grey. Chin, neck and breast are grey, abdomen white. Legs are pink and bill pink with white horny tip. In type the *Grey Lag* is long, narrow and shallow. It is long in the leg and of horizontal carriage but has a proportionately shorter neck than the *Canada*. It is believed that most of our domesticated breeds were bred from the *Grey Lag*.

Sebastopol

The *Sebastopol*, sometimes known as *Danubian*, is a large white goose with long curling feathers on back and wings. It is fairly common in the Black Sea area and is also found in parts of Hungary, the Balkans and in regions of the Lower Danube. It is said to have been first imported into this country after the Crimean War.

Environment

For one or two pairs of duck a very small pen with a small pool will suffice. Individuals in a large collection of waterfowl need space to move about without continually bumping into each other. This is especially necessary if some of the more aggressive varieties such as the foreign shelduck are kept. The ideal breeding ground for all types in a large collection is marsh, good grass and water with natural green feed, such as watercress and duck-weed. Bushes and overhanging branches, reeds and long grass provide natural shelter in hot weather as well as in wind. Swimming water need be only 600 mm or less for surface feeders, whilst diving duck prefer a depth of 1200 mm or more.

Housing is unnecessary but there should be protection against vermin, stray cats and dogs by using 2 m wire netting 4 cm mesh. The bottom edge should be buried below ground level to a depth of 30–40 cm. This also prevents pinioned birds from escaping. If natural shade and shelter is not available the pen can be planted with ornamental shrubs—varieties of Salix grow quickly from cuttings.

One side of a pool should have a slope to the water's edge as pinioned birds are not as nimble as birds which are fully winged, but apart from this, steep sides to a pool act as wind breaks and provide shade. An island helps to give birds a sense of security.

Nest boxes
The pen should be made as natural as possible. Nesting sites should be chosen to be available well before the nesting season. Birds naturally select more than one site before laying so that when special nest boxes have to be provided there should be more than one per breeding pair and so placed to give variety.

The *Carolina* and *Mandarin* usually nest in the hollow trunks of trees so, if possible, a tree stump should be 'planted' at an angle for them to climb up it. About 1–1·2 m off the ground a weatherproof wooden box or barrel with an easily accessible entrance hole about 10 cm square should be securely fixed so that the entrance faces away from visitors to give privacy when laying and sitting. A natural screen should be planted in front of the nest. It is unnecessary to provide nesting material.

For the *Shelduck*, old milk churns or something similar, can be placed horizontally in the ground so that the open end is just visible. Long grass or rushes close to water to form plenty of cover, should be left for birds that nest on the ground—geese, the *Pochard* family, *Pintail*, *Mallard*, *Teal*, etc.

Birds often oblige by nesting in large upturned wooden boxes that have had a portion cut out of one side. In such nests the eggs are safeguarded against birds of prey. If an open nest is visible a natural 'roof' should be placed well above it so that eggs cannot be observed from above.

Feeding

Through most of the year ducks and geese thrive on a grain diet. During the breeding season it is advisable to feed a balanced breeders' ration, such as is used for domestic water fowl. Geese should be fed sparingly to encourage them to graze and some of the duck breeds such as *Widgeon* are also almost entirely grazers. A feed should be given twice daily, morning and evening, sufficient to last for about twenty minutes only so that other birds and vermin are not attracted.

Young stock can be fed on a duckling mash mixed to a crumbly moistness with water, small pellets or crumbs. Green feed such as chopped lettuce, duckweed, lawn mowings of young grass should be given daily. Ducklings of some breeds—such as *Shelduck*—require additional animal protein in the form of live water insects, crustaceans or fish scraps.

Pinioning

Ducklings and goslings can be pinioned to prevent straying by any of the following methods:

- Within one week of hatching remove the end of one wing, severing it at the joint farthest from the body using sharp scissors, knife or razor blade. The joint can be felt between finger and thumb by running along the wing from the tip, or in light coloured ducklings it can be seen by holding the wing up in front of a strong light. The part of the wing removed is the second phalanx (and the very small distal phalanx) of the third digit which carries the primary feathers.
- Cutting off the flight feathers after each moult and before flights are fully grown but leaving a single outer flight for appearance's sake or taping the flights together. Some of the birds are almost sure to stray if these methods are used as it is difficult to catch all birds at exactly the right time.
- Cutting the extensor muscle, which must be done by a veterinary surgeon.

All these methods have the effect of throwing the bird off balance as it attempts to rise into the air, but pinioning does not appear to hurt or harm the bird in any way if done correctly.

Note should be taken of the Statutory Instrument 1974 No 1062, The Welfare of Livestock (Cattle or Poultry) Regulations which came into operation on 1 October 1974.

Prohibited operations include 'Any operation on a bird with the object or effect of impeding its flight'. However these regulations apply only to birds that are livestock for the time being situated on agricultural land within the meaning of the Agriculture (Miscellaneous Provisions) Act 1968. In this Act, livestock is defined as any creature kept for the production of food, wool, skin or fur or for use in the farming of land or for such purposes as the Minister may by order specify; and agricultural land is defined as land used for agriculture 'within the meaning of the Agriculture Act, 1947, or, in Scotland, the Agriculture (Scotland) Act 1948, which is so used for the purpose of a trade or business'. The definition of Agriculture in the 1947 and 1948 Acts includes livestock breeding and keeping and the use of land as grazing or meadow lands.

Incubation

Incubation may be natural or artificial. In the case of artificial incubation in hot-air, natural draught machines, the height of the thermometer should be adjusted to be level with the top of the eggs. Incubators are invaluable when there is a shortage of broody hens or broody bantams but it is desirable to have good 'mothers' available to take over the care of the youngsters when they have hatched.

The more favoured way is to use broody hens or bantams according to size of eggs to be set. If a breeder can find a broody strain of small fowl or bantam he would be well advised to keep his own flock of broodies which he can keep free from parasites and in good health. A good broody shuffles down on to the hand when it is placed beneath her and when an egg is placed before her she tucks it under her with her beak.

A nest box should be placed on the ground for extra moisture and a nest made for the broody by cutting out a piece of turf that will fit inside. This should be beaten to a shallow saucer-shape, dusted with insect powder and lined with soft hay. A few unwanted eggs should be put inside the nest and after giving the broody a feed of grain she should be thoroughly dusted with insect powder under the wings and under the vent, and at dusk moved quietly to the nest box. When she seems to be sitting well, say after 24 hours, she can be allowed out for more grain and a drink (previously placed just in front of her box), and the original eggs replaced by those to be incubated, a note having been made of the date upon which the eggs were set. She should be left sitting for 24 hours and then fed once a day. If the nest box door is open she will come out and help herself, but it is important to free her at the same time of day or she may become restless and damage the eggs. Hand turning of the eggs once a day is necessary since hens are unable to turn large eggs satisfactorily.

Eggs should be as fresh as possible and those of wild breeds should be set as soon as possible after a clutch is complete. If storage conditions are similar, eggs from domesticated breeds can be kept a little longer when set under a hen than in an incubator.

The best type of nest box is one that opens at the front rather than at the top because the broody can walk in carefully to cover the eggs. If the nest box opens at the top she has to jump down amongst the eggs and may crush them.

Before the youngsters hatch, a rearing coop should be ready. This should either have a portable run set inside a portable rearing pen with a wire-netting covered top, or should have a surround of wire netting to form a pen in a position where ducklings or goslings can be easily seen and protected from predators.

Rearing

After they hatch the mother will brood the youngsters until they are completely dry and fluffed up. They should then be placed in a chick box lined with hay, and the mother taken to the rearing coop to be given a feed of grain and water. While she eats and settles down the youngsters may be examined, wing banded and recorded together with any other job needed at this stage, because as they get older they are more difficult to catch and handle. Water, in a jam jar fount, and a first feed, as already described, should be placed just outside the bars of the rearing coop. The ducklings or goslings should then be returned one at a time and placed in front of the broody. If she has been previously tried out she should take them readily enough. If she does not take them the first time, she should be given a little longer to settle down and, failing all else, they should be placed under her after dark. Even so it is well to have a spare broody in reserve for emergencies.

As the birds grow, the size of the water container should be increased until, when feathers start to take the place of down, they can be allowed swimming water (which they may have at an earlier stage if the weather is mild).

The parent duck or goose can of course be allowed to sit on her eggs and there are few more beautiful sights than the mother and ducklings (or goslings) on water. The mother objects to having her brood under cover at night and with very small ducklings they would tend to get trampled on. They are therefore less protected than ducklings under a broody hen at night and during the day the small varieties of duck are less able to protect their offspring from predatory birds.

Maintaining health

Diseases and their prevention

A flock of healthy, thriving birds always show a better profit than one with disease and high mortality. It is of great importance for producers to minimise the risks of infection and promote the health of their flocks by good management.

Recently the knowledge that effective drugs are available to combat disease has consoled many a duck producer but under no circumstances should they be regarded as a substitute for good management; they are merely an adjunct to it.

In the first place, the breeding stock should be as free as possible from disease, and this applies in particular to the salmonella group of organisms which can be transmitted to the progeny. If hatching eggs or stock are bought in they should be obtained from Poultry Health Scheme premises, otherwise an attempt should be made to ensure the vendor's stock is disease free.

Cleanliness

Clean accommodation from the outset helps to give the young birds a good start. As already mentioned (under Incubation) the incubator room and all its equipment should be thoroughly cleaned and disinfected between each hatch. Cleansing and disinfection must continue not only during incubation but through brooding, rearing and fattening; in other words, from the time the duck or goose is hatched until it is killed.

If the land can be well rested between batches the danger from soil-borne infections is reduced. Rotational systems in which land is used for poultry only once every few years are excellent. Light, sandy soil is the ideal, as it tends to harbour less disease and is well drained. Heavy land is not suitable for large-scale duck farming being too wet during the winter months. Excessive manure deposits are not conducive to good health and over-stocking creates this problem. A constant supply of clean water is essential but is not always easy to achieve, as ducks and geese tend to be very messy in both eating and drinking. Regular cleaning of troughs helps. In the past, fowl cholera has occurred where birds have drunk contaminated water and as a precaution against this it is preferable to use piped water only. When ducklings and goslings are small, placing their drinkers on wire frames helps to keep the surrounding areas dry, and if these and the hoppers are regularly moved, bare patches that are still a

67

regrettable feature of many farms are avoided. Incorrect feeding not only produces a poor bird but makes it more prone to disease insomuch as its resistance is lowered. A sick or ailing bird should immediately be removed from the pen but if more than the odd one or two has to be taken out then veterinary advice should be sought and typical specimens sent to a veterinary laboratory for a definite diagnosis. This is important as quick action can prevent further loss.

Preventing disease introduction

Any new stock of either sex purchased in the growing or adult stage should be segregated from the rest of the stock for two or three weeks as a precaution against the possible introduction of disease. Every effort should be made to eliminate rats from premises. They can kill ducklings and goslings but of greater importance can act as carriers of disease such as salmonellosis particularly by the contamination of feed stores. Whenever possible feed stores should be rat proof. Effective poisons are now available which are safer to use than previous ones, but care should be taken when laying bait to see that domestic animals, including poultry, cannot gain access.

Visitors and vehicles entering the farm should be regarded as a possible source of danger. Past experience has shown for instance that a few outbreaks of virus hepatitis have been introduced in this way. Visits should be limited to essentials only and persons who come into contact with livestock should put on a full set of outer protective clothing maintained on the premises for that purpose. Loading points for vehicles should be provided well away from the livestock units. Supplies of disinfectant for personal and vehicle disinfection should always be maintained.

Because certain infections of turkeys and chickens may be transmitted by ducks and geese it is desirable to ensure that there is strict segregation of the different species.

Disinfection

As a routine measure all movable equipment should be taken outside and if large tanks are available soaking helps a great deal in removing caked material. If the unit is a small one, scrubbing by hand can be done, but where big areas are involved the most convenient and labour saving method is by the use of vacuum cleaners, high pressure washers and steam cleaners. Such equipment if intelligently handled is effective and efficient.

The cleaning operation must be applied to the whole house at the same time and can be divided as follows:

- All over preliminary spray with disinfectant solution to lay the dust and prevent spread of any infection.
- Removal of movable equipment as mentioned above.
- Removal of litter.
- Cleansing of walls, ventilators, etc and removal of scrapings.
- Disinfection of clean surfaces to kill any organisms.

- Return of clean disinfected equipment to the building.
- Whole house fumigation where practicable.
- Leaving the building empty for as long as possible before restocking.

More detailed information on the cleansing process, the types of chemical disinfectants available for specific purposes, and on fumigation is contained in Advisory Leaflet 514.*

To keep down the level of contamination it is now a practice on some farms to use mist generators whilst the house is occupied by stock. It is claimed that advantages are to be gained by this form of disinfectant dispersal, provided the material used is designed for this specific purpose. It must be emphasised that proper cleansing and disinfection is possible only when a house has been emptied of livestock, and that 'fogging' is no substitute for the kind of complete disinfection procedure outlined above.

The general rule applying to the use of all disinfectants, chemical or other wise, is to follow the recommendation of the manufacturer at all times.

Diseases

Infectious diseases of ducks and geese are principally of importance in areas where large numbers are raised annually, particularly on farms where successive batches of ducklings are introduced at frequent intervals. Although severe infestations with external parasites, intestinal worms and blood parasites seldom occur in Britain, both ducks and geese are susceptible hosts for many parasites.

Duck virus hepatitis

Virus hepatitis is a highly infectious disease of ducklings. It is also known to cause losses in young *Mallard* ducks both in the wild state and when domesticated. Chickens and turkeys on infected farms are not susceptible to disease and goslings are resistant.

At least two forms of the disease are known to occur in this country. The original Type I, or classical form is characterised by its sudden onset and rapid, violent course, and in ducklings under three weeks old, up to 90 per cent may be dead within two days of the first losses. Resistance to Type I infection increases rapidly with increasing age, so that losses in ducklings infected at four weeks of age seldom exceed five per cent and death is rare in ducks over five weeks old.

The Type II form of the disease, which was first seen in Norfolk in the autumn of 1963, is characterised by its lower mortality rate and by its ability to affect older ducklings. Thus mortality seldom exceeds 50–60 per cent but may be delayed until the third, fourth, fifth or even sixth week of life.

At the present time Type II infection appears to be rare but further experience may show the proportion of outbreaks due to the two types to vary from one year to another

*Advisory Leaflet 514 *The Disinfection and Disinfestation of Poultry Houses*. Single copies can be obtained free from the Ministry of Agriculture, Fisheries and Food, (Publications), Tolcarne Drive, Pinner, Middlesex HA5 2DT.

Symptoms

With Type I infection the first deaths may occur within 24 hours of exposure. The disease spreads rapidly through an infected group and practically all losses occur within two to three days of the first deaths. Often the biggest ducklings are first to die sometimes without warning and others may die within thirty minutes of the onset of symptoms. Affected ducklings become dull, cease eating and fail to keep up with the others. Within a short time they fall on their sides with heads drawn back and paddle spasmodically with their feet. The bill is often congested and purple in colour. Sick ducklings continue to drink and may pass green watery excreta. Some affected ducklings make a rapid and complete recovery and may not be noticeably lighter at eight weeks than those that avoided infection.

With Type II infection losses usually commence three to four days after exposure to infection, eg, three to four days after being put on to an infected field. The symptoms are similar to those described above.

Transmission

There is no conclusive evidence that the virus can be transmitted through the hatching egg. It is believed that infection normally occurs through the bird eating infective material. The virus appears in the excreta within a few hours of infection and the disease then spreads very rapidly through an affected group. The virus can live in infected litter, brooders, etc. for many weeks and in this way may cause disease in successive batches. In addition it may be carried from infected to healthy groups on crates, vehicles, barrows or on the hands and clothes of attendants, etc. or transmitted from farm to farm by starlings and other wild birds. Confirmation of the diagnosis can be made by laboratory tests.

Hygiene and isolation

Although workers have reported that the virus can be transmitted through the hatching egg, there is as yet no evidence that this is of practical importance under farm conditions. Thus day-old ducklings put into clean buildings or brooders invariably remain free of infection unless this is introduced from outside.

Many owners have in fact been able to avoid infection in housed ducklings in this way. Unfortunately, however, these birds have still been susceptible to Type II infection when transferred to the fattening units at three, four or even five weeks of age. Thus this method of control is not sufficient by itself unless clean fattening units, well away from any infected ducks can also be provided.

Isolation is obviously easier if the brooding premises are some distance away from the fattening unit and have separate attendants. A logical extension of this idea is to farm out to a specialist rearer the task of rearing the ducklings to three to four weeks of age. In either case care must be taken not to introduce infection on crates, boots, clothing etc. when ducklings are being moved to the fattening units. The buildings used for young ducklings should also be screened against wild birds.

If possible the brooding premises should consist of a number of separate units rather than a single shed so if infection is introduced, it should be possible to stamp it out by thorough cleaning and disinfection of the affected unit without having to depopulate the whole site.

Although buildings can be effectively disinfected to give a clean start it is obviously impossible to disinfect a contaminated fattening field. Usually, however, a rest period of six months is sufficient for the infection to die out. Wherever possible control by hygiene and isolation should be supported by the vaccination of newly hatched ducklings as described under 'Immunisation—the use of vaccine'.

Immunisation—the use of serum
Serum prepared from blood collected from survivors at the time of slaughter for table contains protective antibodies. This serum injected into all ducklings of a group in which losses are just commencing reduces mortality, but unfortunately there are practical difficulties involved in the general application of this method.

Immunisation—the use of vaccine
A vaccine has proved very effective in controlling Type I infection. Inoculation is usually carried out by stabbing the foot web of newly hatched ducklings. Alternatively, the breeding stock can be injected with vaccine so that they produce protective antibodies that are passed through the egg to the duckling. (Plate IV).

At the present time (1978) it is difficult to advise on vaccination against Type II infection. A vaccine similar to that used against Type I infection has been developed but is not yet available for general use. Under the circumstances it is suggested that owners should ask the local Divisional Veterinary Officer of the Ministry's Animal Health Division for advice on the use of the various vaccines available.

Duck plague

Duck plague, otherwise known as duck virus enteritis, is not to be confused with duck virus hepatitis. It is a disease that has been known to exist in parts of Europe for at least thirty years. More recently it has been confirmed in India and the United States. The first outbreak occurred in this country in 1972 when there were four isolated outbreaks.

Signs
The first signs of the disease in a flock may simply be that birds are found dead, floating in the water. Sometimes the birds are seen to be ill; they may have drooping wings and seem reluctant to move or take to the water. Diarrhoea, causing a matting of the vent feathers is sometimes a feature. There may also be a dirty appearance about the head due to increased secretion from the eyes and nostrils. Occasionally in adult male birds the penis may be found protruding after death but this is not diagnostic. Very heavy losses may be experienced in flocks of all ages.

Diagnosis
A post-mortem examination is necessary before a diagnosis of duck plague can be made. Sometimes a straightforward examination leads to a confident diagnosis but on other occasions it may be necessary to make microscopical examinations and virological tests.

Prevention and control
The disease is caused by a virus which affects all members of the Order Anseriformes. Domestic fowls and turkeys are not affected. The most likely way for waterfowl to become infected is by migrating birds bringing the virus with them. It follows that if a flock can be kept away from migrating wild fowl there is a good chance of preventing them becoming diseased.

It has been noted that duck plague is more likely to spread if the birds have access to water. Furthermore, if the water is flowing it is more likely that the disease will spread downstream rather than upstream. Therefore, in the event of an outbreak, or at a time of great risk, there is less chance of spreading the disease within a flock if the birds are kept on dry land.

There is no specific treatment for diseased birds. It is possible to prevent the disease occurring by vaccination and supplies of a licensed vaccine are held at the Animal Health Trust Laboratory, Newmarket, Suffolk, and would be released in an emergency with the agreement of MAFF.

Newcastle disease
(Fowl Pest)

Newcastle disease is a notifiable disease under the Fowl Pest Order of 1936. When its presence is suspected the fact must be reported without delay to a police officer.

Ducks and geese may become infected with Newcastle disease virus and be able to pass it on to chicks and other birds. In general they are unlikely to develop obvious symptoms of the disease but cases have been recorded in ducks where the disease caused a drop in egg production and the birds went into a moult.

Anatipestifer infection

(Known also as Duck Septicaemia, New Duck Disease and *Infectious Serositis*)
Anatipestifer infection is an infectious disease of ducklings caused by a bacterial organism. It was first described on Long Island, America, in 1932, where it has become the most important disease problem affecting ducks; in England it is known to occur in several counties. Growing ducklings of four to nine weeks old are affected but the disease may spread back to ducklings of brooder age or to older groups. Adult ducks are resistant but losses in susceptible age groups can range from three per cent under good husbandry conditions to 75 per cent under conditions of environmental stress. Under adverse conditions other bacterial diseases such as E. coli septicaemia, Salmonellosis and

Pasteurellosis may cause concurrent losses and complicate diagnosis and control measures.

Incubation period and course
The incubation period varies from less than 36 hours to five days. Death may occur within a few hours of the onset of symptoms but in older groups it may follow an illness of six to seven days. Some ducks may survive but remain culls.

Even when uncomplicated by other infections, the disease may occur as a severe spreading condition affecting almost all ducklings in susceptible groups and causing mortality of up to 75 per cent. In some flocks the disease may be milder with lower mortality; in others it may occur as a sporadic condition affecting a few of the flock only.

Symptoms
Affected ducklings show many of the symptoms associated with Newcastle disease in chickens. There is usually a watery discharge from the eyes and nostrils. Dullness with loss of appetite is accompanied by a green diarrhoea, the feathers around the vent being stained green. Affected birds rapidly become weak and may be unable to stand; if stimulated they cry out as if in pain and stagger away a few paces before flopping down or toppling over. There may be a continuous nervous movement of the head and neck or bobbing of the tail.

Ducks which survive for a few days may develop permanent nervous symptoms and die as a result of being unable to get feed and water. Those less severely affected lose condition, develop a staggering gait and the plumage becomes dirty and ragged. The hock joints may become swollen. Diagnosis is based upon the history, symptoms and post mortem findings, if possible confirmed by a bacteriological examination.

Method of infection
Early experimental work suggested that infection entered the body through small skin wounds especially those on the feet, but the germ Pasteurella (formerly Pfeifferella) anatipestifer causing the disease does not survive long in droppings or soil. Consequently the current opinion is that a few ducklings carry the infection in the upper respiratory tract from whence it spreads to the lungs and air sacs under conditions of stress, such as over-crowding in damp cold weather. Spread from bird to bird might be via the drinking water or through the inhalation of infected dust or droplets of nasal discharge.

Control
The first aim should be to provide a correct environment for rearing ducklings, ie control of temperature and ventilation in intensive rearing houses, and careful hardening off in the case of ducklings moving outside where there should be shelter and windbreaks.

Although true egg transmission has not been proven it would seem wise to exclude wild waterfowl from the breeding pens and to maintain a high standard of hatchery hygiene.

Treatment
Ducks showing severe symptoms do not respond to treatment. Within the usual age range of four to nine weeks the most effective treatment is the single intra-muscular injection of 83 mg each of streptomycin and dihydrostreptomycin using a commercial preparation such as 'Dimycin-V' (Glaxo) containing this quantity per 0·5 ml of injectable solution. Ducklings less than three weeks of age should receive half this dose. Medication of the drinking water with sulphadimidine sodium at a level of 30–60 g per 100 birds per day for three days is also effective. Water medication using a rimethorim (eight per cent) sulpha-diazine (40 per cent) mixture, given for three to five days at a level of 1 ml/litre of drinking water is especially effective if started in anticipation of the problem or very early in the disease. Medication of the feed with sulphaquinoxaline at a level of 125 mg/kg has proved useful in reducing losses and will also prevent coccidiosis.

Salmonellosis
(Also known as paratyphoid)
The term salmonellosis is used to describe the bacterial disease caused by any member of the group of salmonella except *S pullorum*, the cause of pullorum disease, and *S gallinarum* the cause of fowl typhoid. The disease usually occurs during the first few days of life, particularly when infection has occurred in the incubator. Salmonellosis is common in ducklings and is frequently referred to as Keel disease.

The types of Salmonellae most commonly involved are *S typhimurium*, *S enteritidis* and *S anatum*. All three infections can act as the primary cause of disease or, more commonly, can be secondary to some other disease factor. *S typhimurium* is important in public health as being a cause of food poisoning in man. Goslings are also susceptible to Salmonellosis.

Symptoms
Symptoms are similar to those seen in *S pullorum* disease in chicks. Ducklings suffering from loss of appetite and diarrhoea tend to remain near the warmth of the brooder often fall forwards on to their breasts and have difficulty in rising. Birds may be found dead without having shown symptoms of illness. Bacteriological examination is essential for diagnosis and several carcases should be sent to a veterinary laboratory for this purpose.

Transmission
Most types of salmonellae occurring in birds are also found in other domesti-cated animals and man. Rats and mice are often carriers of salmonellae and their droppings can contaminate poultry feed. Feeding incubator waste, infertile eggs, eggshell grit or swill containing poultry offal may introduce the infection if these products have not been heat-treated in a MAFF approved manner. Secondhand incubators, brooders etc. should always be thoroughly disinfected before use. Some ducklings which survive an outbreak become 'carriers' and the organisms may be excreted in the droppings for a period of many months, although some birds eliminate the infection much sooner. If there is faecal

contamination of the shell of eggs laid by these 'carriers' and the organisms remain alive, they can penetrate the shell during incubation and multiply within the egg. In the duck it is not uncommon for salmonellae to be present in the droppings or intestinal contents and consequently infection can enter the egg soon after it has been laid. It is also possible that infection may be present in that part of the oviduct where the shell is formed and once again this type of infection would be difficult to distinguish from a true ovarian infection. Once salmonellae are inside the egg they are protected from washing or fumigation and the ducklings which hatch out are likely to be infected. The contamination of eggs with salmonellae such as *S typhimurium* which commonly cause human food poisoning represents, of course, a potential danger to public health.

Prevention and control
Every effort should be made to obtain clean eggs by providing clean well-bedded nests. Eggs should be gathered as early as possible after the breeders finish laying and should be washed or fumigated. Hatching eggs should never be soaked in cold water and wiped with a dirty cloth since this will help to spread the infection.

Furazolidone has been found to be effective in reducing mortality, but as some of the treated birds remain 'carriers' of the infection they should not be retained for breeding stock. The presence of a group of survivors represents a focus of infection, and the disease may spread on the farm. Dead or culled ducklings and bedding should be burned and the house and equipment adequately cleaned and disinfected. The related drug nitrofurazone is toxic to ducklings, so care must be taken not to use this, or any preparation containing it, in error for furazolidone.

Pasteurellosis
(Fowl Cholera)
Pasteurellosis is an infectious disease of poultry caused by the organism *Pasteurella multocida* (aviseptica). During the 1930s a severe, rapidly fatal form of Pasteurellosis, with mortality up to 80 or 90 per cent, caused heavy losses among ducks and geese. Fortunately this form of the disease, which is known as 'fowl cholera' is now rare in Great Britain. However, a less severe form of Pasteurellosis is not uncommon as a cause of quite heavy mortality (eg 25 per cent or more) in ducks and geese in the fattening stage. Adult birds are also susceptible.

Symptoms
The disease usually affects flocks of over four weeks of age. Symptoms include loss of appetite, thirst, high body temperature and sudden death. Mucoid white droppings followed by light green droppings are usually seen. Swollen hock joints due to localised infection often occur in the late stages of an outbreak. Mortality may reach 50 per cent or even higher. Positive diagnosis depends on bacteriological examination and carcases from suspected outbreaks should be submitted to a laboratory for examination.

Prevention and control

The outbreak of 'fowl cholera' referred to above was introduced by imported geese. This emphasises the advice given in the previous section that newly purchased stock should be kept in isolation.

If an outbreak of pasteurellosis occurs, the use of high levels of antibiotic in the feed or water eg chlortetracycline (aureomycin) or oxtetracycline (terramycin) at 100 or 200 g/t of feed may be helpful in suppressing the disease and in preventing its spread to healthy birds. Birds that are already sick are unlikely to respond to this medication, and it is advisable either to kill them or to seek veterinary advice with a view to treating them with injections of antibiotic before putting them on to medicated feed or water. Care should be exercised in disposing of all carcases. These should be burnt or efficiently buried and all contact birds should be strictly isolated. Even with these precautions the disease may recur when treatment is discontinued, and one should be prepared to de-populate the premises and to put later hatches of birds on to clean ground well away from the contaminated area. Vaccines are used in some countries but cannot yet be recommended without reservations for use under British conditions.

Erysipelas

Erysipelas is not common in domestic ducks but can cause outbreaks of severe mortality in either the rearing or fattening stage. Laboratory examination is necessary to distinguish between erysipelas and other causes of sudden death.

Aspergillosis

Aspergillosis is a disease affecting many species of wild and domesticated birds and is caused by the fungus *Aspergillus fumigatus*. The disease usually affects ducklings during the first two weeks of life.

Symptoms

Small ducklings may die suddenly without symptoms having been observed. Laboured breathing and other respiratory symptoms, are usually observed in older ducklings and mature ducks.

Prevention

There is no treatment of value. Mouldy straw appears to be the chief source of infection so special care must be given to the selection of bedding for ducklings and in most cases clean wood shavings are preferable. A clean egg-laying environment is also very important and particular attention should be paid to the cleanliness and dryness of materials used in the nest boxes. Cracked eggs are particularly liable to become infected with Aspergillus and should not be used for hatching since they can be an important means of introducing infection into a hatchery and creating problems of hatchery hygiene.

Aflatoxicosis

First recognised as a problem in 1960 when some batches of Brazilian groundnuts caused heavy mortality in farm stock including ducks and turkey.

The condition is due to presence of *Aspergillus flavus* in the groundnut, which, although killed in processing, leaves a toxin (aflatoxin) which causes 'aflatoxicosis' in the susceptible species. Groundnuts from other countries, together with maize, soya and other tropical or sub-tropical feeds, can be infected with the fungus. Other fungi can produce similar toxins but most outbreaks in this country have been associated with groundnuts containing aflatoxin. Ducks are highly susceptible to aflatoxin with affected ducklings showing high mortality. Groundnuts or soya for feeding to ducks should be bought only from reputable sources.

Parasitic diseases

Domestic ducks in Britain are seldom infested with external parasites or worms.

Gizzard worm of geese

This is a small worm, fine as a piece of reddish-brown cotton and from 10–25 mm in length which buries its head in the inner lining of the gizzard.

Old geese have considerable resistance to this worm but young ones lose condition and may die from a heavy infestation. A simple way of detecting small numbers of gizzard worm is to detach the lining of the gizzard and suspend it in a jam jar of clear water. The worms are then clearly visible as they float out from the gizzard lining into the water though remaining attached to the lining in most cases.

Symptoms
Usually the first symptom noticed is a rather slow and staggering gait and the affected gosling is very thin and weak.

Prevention and treatment
As this worm is picked up from infested land the birds should be moved to another field. Changing the birds' range as often as possible is the best way of preventing this trouble.

This worm does not affect geese that have access to a large pond, stream or river. The use of small artificial ponds is not advised because the ground around them can soon become infested. Movable drinkers should always be provided and these should be shifted as often as possible as geese spend much of their time around them and, if their position is not often changed, the surrounding ground becomes severely fouled.

Treatment, which is quite effective, consists of giving a capsule of carbon tetrachloride. For goslings up to 3·6 kg, a 1 ml capsule should be given; over that weight 2 ml is required. Repeat the dose in about seven days time. Birds with this condition need good feeding, and a good layers' mash or boiled grain with a little milk or milk powder should be given, letting the birds eat all they can. Several other drugs are now available which can be used for treatment of this infestation, eg levamisole at a dose of 25 mg/kg body-weight in the drinking water for three days. This drug is much safer than carbon tetrachloride.

77

Polymorphus infection of ducks

This parasite occurs in a variety of wild birds and is frequently present in domestic ducks having access to natural water. On many small farms where ducks have constant access to water a relatively low burden of worms is acquired and no harm results. Where, however, ducks are suddenly released or escape from pens on to water they may acquire a heavy worm burden which causes serious damage to the mucosa of the intestine and may be fatal. Heavily infected birds become stunted, thin and weak, but these effects seem to be due to mechanical damage to the intestine. Ducks become infected by eating fresh-water shrimps in which the worm spends part of its life cycle. There is some evidence that starvation for 48 hours results in the elimination of a large proportion of the worms and carbon tetrachloride at a dose rate of 2 ml/kg of body-weight has been suggested as a treatment. Other effective drugs are also obtainable.

Coccidiosis of ducks

Coccidiosis is not a frequent cause of loss but sporadic outbreaks of disease have been reported. Several types of coccidia occur and all are quite different from the species found in chickens. At least one species may cause acute disease with a high mortality in young ducks. The parasites multiply in the cells lining the intestine where heavy infestations cause inflammation and haemorrhage.

Symptoms
The first symptom of disease is loss of appetite followed by loss of weight and weakness. Haemorrhagic diarrhoea may also be present. Sudden death is a common finding in outbreaks of coccidiosis in young ducks.

Treatment
The acute disease has been controlled successfully using sodium sulphadimidine in the drinking water at 0·1 per cent (half the usually recommended concentration for chickens) in an interrupted treatment consisting of three days on drug, two days on plain water followed by a final period of three days on drug. This condition is relatively uncommon and it would be wise to obtain laboratory confirmation before commencing treatment.

Coccidiosis of geese

Several types of coccidia occur in the intestine of geese but their pathogenicity is uncertain. The most important form of the disease is caused by the rapid multiplication of large numbers of parasites in the cells lining the tubules of the kidney. Under ordinary extensive range conditions the disease is not particularly common but when goslings are reared intensively losses may be serious.

Symptoms
The first symptom usually noticed is diarrhoea with whitish colouration of the faeces. Weakness and emaciation soon follow.

Treatment

Provided that treatment is initiated at an early stage the condition responds to sulphonamides administered in the drinking water according to the manufacturer's instructions.

Leg disorders

These have become an increasing problem as ducklings grow faster and are reared intensively. The causes are uncertain but wire floors have been blamed and it has been claimed that the addition of rich sources of the B vitamins such as dried brewer's yeast sometimes prevents the condition. Genetic factors may also be involved but are only likely to be recognised by the large scale breeder. As with most leg deformities in table birds, treatment of any kind is seldom of any value once the bones or joints have become permanently deformed.

Lameness

Geese are very clumsy and often injure themselves; if caught or held by the legs they may go lame, but unless the leg is broken they soon recover although feeding may be necessary until they can walk again.

Prevention and treatment

Geese should always be caught by the neck to avoid hurting their legs.

Hard cornlike swellings may form on the underside of the feet if the birds are run on dry, hard or uneven ground. These usually clear if the geese are removed to a good pasture or softer, more even ground. If the condition becomes acute, the harder parts may be cut away with a knife and the area dressed with antiseptic.

The attention of those in any way concerned with the keeping of poultry is drawn to the need for regular and effective vaccination against Newcastle Disease. Information and advice may be obtained from the local Divisional Veterinary Officer of MAFF. Addresses are in local telephone directories.

Codes of recommendations for the welfare of livestock (as provided for in Section 3 of the Agriculture (Miscellaneous Provisions) Act 1978) are approved by Parliament and published. Should such a Code be approved by Parliament for ducks or geese and differences occur between the advice given here and that Code, the latter will prevail.

Appendix 1

Preparing oven-ready birds

● Remove the sinews by cutting just through the scaly skin around the legs about 2·5 cm below the hock. Break the bone where the cut was made, and if the foot is pulled away from the leg the sinews will come away with it. This is not always done with ducks as they are killed when they are very young.

● Cut between the large wing bones and discard the end part.

● Place the bird breast downwards with the head hanging over the edge of the table. Three-quarters of the way from shoulders to neck (about 12–15 cm) make an incision across it of about 2·5 cm. Pick up the skin on the shoulder side of the cut between finger and thumb and cut a strip 2·5 cm wide back to the shoulders. Cut through the head end of the neck and the rest of the skin where *the original cut* was made and discard the head. Cut off the narrow strip of skin just above the shoulders. Clear the neck and large flap of skin, of tissue including the crop and wind pipe and cut off the neck at the shoulders. Turn back the large flap over the neck cavity.

● Place the bird on the palm of the left hand using the second finger of the right hand to loosen the lungs which are embedded in the ribs near the backbone.

● With the bird resting on its shoulder make an incision between the vent and the 'parson's nose', this exposes the intestine which should be hooked with the first finger of the left hand. By inserting the knife beside the finger and between the intestine and the uncut skin the vent can be cut round.

● Place the bird on its back with the tail towards your right. First remove the fat around the abdomen then put the right hand inside the body and grasp the gizzard and give a slow and sustained pull which should result in the complete contents of the abdominal and thoracic cavity (including the lungs) coming out in one piece.

● Keep the heart, gizzard, neck and liver and clean off surplus blood and fat. The gizzard of a duck is difficult to clean as the internal lining is tough, and it adheres tightly to the inner surface. If the gizzard is cut open and the contents removed it will be easier to remove this lining after immersion in boiling water for a few seconds. The gall bladder is very bitter and care should be taken not to break it when it is cut away from the liver.

● The bird is now ready to truss. A 250 mm needle with string is required.

● Pull the flap of skin on the neck back over the neck cavity, lay the bird on its back with tail end towards you and push the legs forward and press them down

on to the table whilst passing the needle through the top of the thigh, through the body, through the other thigh and across the neck. Tie the two ends tightly.
● Pass the needle through the skin just below the end of the breastbone, and then cross the string under the legs and tie firmly behind the 'parson's nose'. This will cover up the hole made for the removal of the intestines and other viscera.

Appendix 2

Temperature conversion

The central figures in bold type refer to the temperatures, either in degrees Centigrade or degrees Fahrenheit, which require conversion. The corresponding temperatures in degrees Fahrenheit or degrees Centigrade will be found to the right or left respectively.

°C		°F	°C		°F
−17·8	0	32·0	− 1·1	30	86·0
−17·2	1	33·8	− 0·6	31	87·8
−16·7	2	35·6	0·0	32	89·6
−16·1	3	37·4	0·6	33	91·4
−15·6	4	39·2	1·1	34	93·2
−15·0	5	41·0	1·7	35	95·0
−14·4	6	42·8	2·2	36	96·8
−13·9	7	44·6	2·8	37	98·6
−13·3	8	46·4	3·3	38	100·4
−12·8	9	48·2	3·9	39	102·2
−12·2	10	50·0	4·4	40	104·0
−11·7	11	51·8	5·0	41	105·8
−11·1	12	53·6	5·6	42	107·6
−10·6	13	55·4	6·1	43	109·4
−10·0	14	57·2	6·7	44	111·2
− 9·4	15	59·0	7·2	45	113·0
− 8·9	16	60·8	7·8	46	114·8
− 8·3	17	62·6	8·3	47	116·6
− 7·8	18	64·4	8·9	48	118·4
− 7·2	19	66·2	9·4	49	120·2
− 6·7	20	68·0	10·0	50	122·0
− 6·1	21	69·8	10·6	51	123·8
− 5·6	22	71·6	11·1	52	125·6
− 5·0	23	73·4	11·7	53	127·4
− 4·4	24	75·2	12·2	54	129·2
− 3·9	25	77·0	12·8	55	131·0
− 3·3	26	78·8	13·3	56	132·8
− 2·8	27	80·6	13·9	57	134·6
− 2·2	28	82·4	14·4	58	136·4
− 1·7	29	84·2	15·0	59	138·2

°C		°F	°C		°F
15·6	60	140·0	27·2	81	177·8
16·1	61	141·8	27·8	82	179·6
16·7	62	143·6	28·3	83	181·4
17·2	63	145·4	28·9	84	183·2
17·8	64	147·2	29·4	85	185·0
18·3	65	149·0	30·0	86	186·8
18·9	66	150·8	30·6	87	188·6
19·4	67	152·6	31·1	88	190·4
20·0	68	154·4	31·7	89	192·2
20·6	69	156·2			
			32·2	90	194·0
21·1	70	158·0	32·8	91	195·8
21·7	71	159·8	33·3	92	197·6
22·2	72	161·6	33·9	93	199·4
22·8	73	163·4	34·4	94	201·2
23·3	74	165·2	35·0	95	203·0
23·9	75	167·0	35·6	96	204·8
24·4	76	168·8	36·1	97	206·6
25·0	77	170·6	36·7	98	208·4
25·6	78	172·4	37·2	99	210·2
26·1	79	174·2			
			37·8	100	212·0
26·7	80	176·0			

Appendix 3

Further reading and information

Publications

Bulletin No 148. *Incubation and Hatchery Practice*. Price £1·75 (net). Obtainable from HMSO. See back cover of this bulletin.

Bulletin No. 174. *Poultry Nutrition*. Price £2·25 (net). Obtainable from HMSO. See back cover of this bulletin.

The Inheritance of Plumage Colour in the Common Duck by F M Lancaster. Published by Martinus Nijhoff, The Hague.

Embryonic Development in the Eggs of the Pekin Duck by R S Kaltofen. Published by the Centre of Agricultural Publishing and Documentation, Wageningen.

Reports on Duck Research carried out by New York State College of Agriculture in co-operation with Long Island Duck Research Co-operative and New York State Veterinary College. Obtainable from Cornell University Duck Research Laboratories, Eastport, Long Island, New York.

The Farmer's Bulletin No 767 *Goose Raising*. Animal and Poultry Husbandry Research Service, USDA.

Bulletin No 532 *Duck and Goose Raising*.

Bulletin No 848 *Raising Geese Bulletin*.

Both obtainable from Information Division, Dept of Agriculture, Ottowa, Ontario.

Profitable Duck Management by M/s J M Hunter and John C Scholes, Beacon Milling Company, Cayuga, New York.

Organisations

The Duck Producers Association, High Holborn House, 52–54 High Holborn, London WC1V 6SX. This is of interest to commercial duck producers.

The Wildfowl Trust, Slimbridge, Gloucestershire GL2 7BT.

The Wildfowlers Association of Great Britain and Ireland (WAGBI)—John Anderton (Director), Marford Mill, Rossett, Clwyd LL12 0HL.

The British Water Fowl Association, Secretary—Mr Christopher J Harrisson, Bell House, 111/113 Lambeth Road, London SE1.

The Game Conservancy, Fordingbridge, Hampshire.

The Norfolk Naturalists Trust, 72 The Close, Norwich.

These organisations and many individuals, have been instrumental in preserving some of our rarer species and their habitats and a debt of gratitude is owed to them.

Printed in the UK for HMSO by Hobbs the Printers of Southampton
(3129) Dd738295 C15 2/86 G3379